CONCILIUM

D1567714

CONCILIUM 2004/4

JOB'S GOD

Edited by
Ellen van Wolde

SCM Press · London

Published by SCM Press, 9–17 St Albans Place, London N1 0NX

Copyright © Stichting Concilium

English translations copyright © 2004 SCM-Canterbury Press Ltd

ISBN 0 334 030803

Printed by Biddles Ltd, www.biddles.co.uk

Concilium Published February, April, June, October
December

Contents

III. Job: Questions around the World

Introduction:
Questions about a World without Justice

ELLEN VAN WOLDE

The book of Job is known for its courageous hero who does not give up discussing God because God has struck him with so many disasters. What kind of God is it who allows good people to suffer so much and who lets wicked people live their comfortable lives? And come to that, what kind of a world is it in which no balance and justice can be found? Why hasn't God developed a design and strategy to take better care of his creatures and their behaviour?

Job confronts his friends and God with this kind of question, questions that are still ours. Perhaps we are less inclined to be as persistent as he is. Possibly we might have given in or might have given up God altogether. Why do we need a God when he isn't helping us? What can a world without a righteous God offer us but that world itself? In order to receive an answer to these problems, Job wants to converse with God himself, because his own friends are worthless. He even finishes suing God in a legal case with God as the defendant. However, when Job finally meets God, it is not in the courtroom but in a thunderstorm.

In his whirlwind speech God gives an impressive account of his competence as creator and steward monitoring the universe and living beings on earth. His creation appears not only to be an action performed at the beginning but to happen every day anew; every morning an immense diversity becomes manifest both in the cosmos and on earth. Observing the skies, all kinds of stars and constellations become visible: sun, moon, planets, constellations, the Milky Way, all stars and systems in endless varieties. Observing the earth, different kinds of animal life become visible: the lion, the raven, the mountain goat, the wild ass and the wild ox, the ostrich, the horse and the eagle; it displays varied wild life in endless species. God's speech is specific, varied and sustainable, in both life and death. No human idea is present of balance or equilibrium, of simple justice and righteousness. Nor is any general wisdom defended or a general rule that explains everything.

Confronted with this broad picture, Job is overwhelmed. But does he also receive an answer to his questions? Is it suggested that human beings such as Job, who cannot have the same overview as God, should give up asking questions altogether? Or does it imply that they should decide for a strict separation between the heavens and the earth? Mightn't they and we join in with Psalm 115.16 which says, 'The heavens belong to the Lord, but the earth he gave over to human beings'? Is this the solution the book of Job offers? If we are led to conclude that God's domain is of a completely different order from the human domain, then human beings themselves are the only ones responsible for their actions and for what happens on earth. Consequently, we cannot blame God for what is going wrong on earth. Moreover, if the variety and diversity on earth is so immense, we cannot arrange it according to our simple rules of justice.

This kind of question and answer is the topic of this issue of *Concilium*. In the first section the positions taken in the book of Job itself will be studied: the way God is depicted in the beginning, middle and ending of the book of Job and how he relates to retribution and justice. A variety of images of God will emerge: Job's and his views that show a certain development, his friends' images of God, and even the Satan's and God's own ideas will be scrutinized. So much is said about God in the book of Job, and will be said here. The second section deals with the philosophical, theological and ethical consequences of what is described above and of the problems and answers in the book of Job. The articles in the third and last section reflect on the way in which Job's questions are faced around the modern world. Starting with the views in Tolkien's *The Lord of the Rings*, so well-known now after being filmed, it will proceed with some Job-like questions raised in the present day's situation in Central America and in South Africa. In fact the closing article in the issue returns to the opening article, in that the opening article reads the problem of retribution and justice in Job 1–3 from a textual, and therefore theoretical, perspective, whereas the last article reads and discusses these very same aspects of Job 1–3 in the South African context of HIV/AIDS. The interaction between these and the other articles will become clear as soon as you start reading.

I. The Book of Job

With or Without a Cause:
Images of God and Man in Job 1–3

ALBERT KAMP

Image is everything nowadays. The way we look, dress, act, talk and the things we talk about, all contribute to the image by which we are perceived and valued by others. It is important to wear the right clothes, talk the talk or walk the walk. The daily facts of social interaction define our outward appearances and at the same time influence our inner perceptions. The way we think about ourselves as human beings is strongly affected by the reactions and especially the judgment of others. On a much larger scale this personal and social image is even intertwined with our world-views and religious beliefs. What is my place within the order of the world? How do my actions take part in the grand scheme of life?

Such present-day existential questions do not differ that much from those in the book of Job. The story of Job focuses on different aspects of human perception of the world and on the way in which people perceive themselves and each other. Right from the beginning readers are introduced to Job's acts and attitude, and not long thereafter his behaviour is appraised by God in heaven, but questioned by one of the heavenly beings, Satan. The very image of Job, be it externally or internally determined, changes as a result of the subsequent divine interventions. And at the same time different, even conflicting world-views come to the fore.

I shall be exploring the opening chapters of the book of Job and focusing on the way the text presents several images of Job, God and Satan and their mutual relationships, which give way to subject-bound perspectives on reality and to divergent world-views.[1]

I. The introduction of Job

It all starts with the following characterization of Job.[2]

> There was once a man in the land of Uz whose name was Job. That man
> was blameless and upright, one who feared God and turned away from
> evil (1.1).

After the scene-setting information about Job's place of origin and his name
the narrator establishes a detailed image of Job, a man who is exemplary in
his moral and religious conduct.[3] Measured by his prosperity and many
riches Job has everything one could wish for: seven sons, three daughters, an
abundance of cattle and many servants. He is indeed 'the greatest of all the
people of the east' (1.3). The enumeration of personal data activates the idea
that there appears to be a certain connection between Job's nature and his
wealth, as if the narrator suggests that Job's prosperity is the result of
his piety.[4] Because of his blameless and honourable nature and because of
his fear for God and his aversion to evil all works well for Job. To illustrate
this specific attitude the narrator presents a recurrent pattern of religious
conduct:

> His sons used to go and hold feasts in one another's houses in turn; and
> they would send and invite their three sisters to eat and drink with them.
> And when the feast days had run their course, Job would send and
> sanctify them, and he would rise early in the morning and offer burnt
> offerings according to the number of them all; for Job said, 'It may be that
> my children have sinned, and cursed God in their hearts.' This is what
> Job always did (1.4–5).

Whenever his children had had a party, the next morning Job cleansed them
from possible sins. These verses reveal that the narrator knows Job inside
out by showing his actions and explaining his reasons. He thus suggests a
relationship between Job's scrupulous behaviour and his prosperity. Job is
afraid that his sons may have cursed God and that this may obscure his
relationship with God.[5]

Consequently, at the very start of the book of Job a connection is created
between Job's attitude and his prosperity, and more generally between
human behaviour and success in life. In this way a specific framework of
causality is activated, and in this setting prosperity is considered to be the
result of a religious attitude. The concept of divine retribution, a *quid pro quo*

or 'something in return', lays the foundation of this framework.[6] It determines Job's habitual actions. In order to maintain his relation with God, Job offers burnt-offerings beforehand, even before he knows for certain that his sons have sinned. He expects, it seems, to affect God's behaviour in reaction to his sons' wrong-doings. The pattern of causality therefore involves two interrelated directions. Not only do divine reward or punishment exert influence on Job's actions but human conduct exerts influence on God's actions. Each end of the relationship is thought of as dependent on the other.

The image of Job presented, as the most perfect man in the east, is intrinsically bound up with an image of God as an almighty judge, who discerns between good and evil and decides on reward and punishment accordingly. The way in which Job thinks, acts and reacts is bound up with this framework of retribution. However, God's perspective is not yet revealed.

II. The divine perspective

A change in scenery directs the reader's attention towards a major change in perspective. From a familiar context on earth the story continues in heaven with a remarkable exchange between God and Satan (1.6–12; 2.1–7). The image of Job's impeccable behaviour already activated seems very much appreciated by God:

> YHWH said to Satan, 'Have you considered my servant Job? There is no one like him on the earth, a blameless and upright man who fears God and turns away from evil' (1.8).

Apart from a literal confirmation of Job's attitude, the image of God in relation to man is consolidated as well. God's position is one of interdependence, once he calls Job his servant. So, the concept of divine retribution still seems valid. However, Satan's reply shakes things up.

> Then Satan answered YHWH, 'Does Job fear God for nothing? Have you not put a fence around him and his house and all that he has, on every side? You have blessed the work of his hands, and his possessions have increased in the land. But stretch out your hand now, and touch all that he has, and he will curse you to your face' (1.9–11).

The image of Job which Satan presents is truly a *quid pro quo*: in his opinion

Job's behaviour originates from God's actions. Job's life, his prosperity and wealth, are the result of God's protection, for God blessed the work of Job's hands. No wonder Job fears God, for he could lose it all. With his question 'Does Job fear God for nothing?' Satan redirects this pattern of thinking to a model of *sine causa* or 'without a cause'. Thus he introduces a hypothetical script in which the crucial 'cause' is omitted. How will Job react when the causal foundation in his relationship with God is wiped away? Will he still fear God when he does not receive any reward?

God's approval of the script indicates a major change in attitude: 'Very well, all that he has is in your power; only do not stretch out your hand against him!' (1.12). Although God approves of Job's conduct, and despite their good relationship in the past, God can act and change his position as he likes. Because of this alteration, the image of God changes as things develop. The events that will take place on earth are, from a human point of view, without any reason, and the disasters that will strike are inexplicable. From a heavenly point of view, however, God's actions have a reason. His consent to Satan's proposal is prompted by a certain inner pride: 'Have you considered my servant Job? There is no one like him.' His very relationship with Satan, and not that with Job, causes God to react in a certain manner.

Until now, the consequence of the heavenly conversation for the human party is a test of the causal foundation of Job's behaviour, and this implies, above all, a change in perspective. Within the boundaries of a divine world-view, retribution is not necessary and the logic of causality does not necessarily apply to God's actions. People's world-views and religious beliefs depend on God, but God does not depend on their views, beliefs and actions.

III. Back to earth

A succession of disasters on earth results from the heavenly conversation: four times in a row a messenger informs Job about the calamities that destroy his good fortune. He loses all his cattle; all servants are killed and his children as well. Striking as it may be, this context of bad luck once again clarifies Job's perspective. In reaction to the deadly scenario Job holds on to his habitual piety:

> Then Job arose, tore his robe, shaved his head, and fell on the ground and worshipped. He said, 'Naked I came from my mother's womb, and naked shall I return there; YHWH gave and YHWH has taken away; blessed be the name of YHWH.' In all this Job did not sin or charge God with wrong-doing (1.20–22).

Job's faith and trust, shown in word and deed, indeed confirm his previous image. He truly fears God. The contents of his speech reflect that he is a true believer. This still fits in with a religious world-view based on causality: God gives and God takes away. Although Job's words suggest an adoption of the divine perspective and an explanation of the events as *sine causa*, he holds on to his human way of thinking in causal patterns. God is still the ultimate cause of the events on earth. This is in conformity with the statement of one of the messengers (1.16): 'The fire of God fell from heaven and burned up the sheep and the servants, and consumed them; I alone have escaped to tell you.' The conversation in heaven already made it clear that the origin of the disasters is Satan, commissioned by God. From a religious human point of view, however, the answer is: who could cause such an event but God? After all, he is the ultimate cause.

Satan's original aim of testing whether Job fears God for nothing seems to have failed. The only thing that has changed so far in Job's opinion is the aspect of retribution, for the occurrences are not explained as divine reward or punishment. He just accepts the events without any complaints and perseveres in his faith in God. He neither blames God nor loses his trust in the principle of causality.

So a second round in heaven and on earth is needed. This time Job's personal health is at stake:

YHWH said to Satan, 'Have you considered my servant Job? There is no one like him on the earth, a blameless and upright man who fears God and turns away from evil. He still persists in his integrity, although you incited me against him, to destroy him for no reason.' Then Satan answered YHWH, 'Skin for skin! All that people have they will give to save their lives. But stretch out your hand now and touch his bone and his flesh, and he will curse you to your face.' YHWH said to Satan, 'Very well, he is in your power; only spare his life' (2.3–6).

The second dialogue in heaven displays a much more personal touch. God not only holds on to his pride regarding Job, but he accuses Satan as well. His words consolidate Satan's position as the cause of his own behaviour and he does not seem content with acting for no reason: 'You incited me against him, to destroy him for no reason.'

Satan's second proposal to God stresses another aspect of the test. Instead of the previous 'for nothing' or 'without a cause', Job's personal piety is accentuated. Will he curse God to his face? In the Hebrew text the tension of this change is even more present, since the same word is used to denote the act of cursing as was used for the act of blessing.[7] It no longer focuses on the reasons for Job's conduct but on his relationship to God. The impeccable image of Job itself is challenged. Job is therefore inflicted with loathsome sores on his whole body. But even the protest of Job's wife cannot, for the time being, change his faith:

> Then his wife said to him, 'Do you still persist in your integrity? Curse God, and die.' But he said to her, 'You speak as any foolish woman would speak. Shall we receive the good at the hand of God, and not receive the bad?' In all this Job did not sin with his lips (2.9–10).

Job holds on to the principles of causality and to his piety at the same time. It may well be that God does not react to human actions in a retributive fashion, but the relationship between human beings and God depends on divine interventions. There is a cause for Job's personal situation in life, but he can no longer influence the divine. His existence, his prosperity and wealth, his health, depend, in his view, on God's grace. Job's attitude of deliverance is piety at its best, as is fully expressed in Job 28.28: 'The fear of the Lord, that is wisdom, and to shun evil is understanding.'[8]

Then Job's wife confronts him with a completely different solution when she says 'Curse God and die'. This seems to confirm Satan's expectations. Why hold on to the relationship, any relationship, with God if misery is your reward? Why worship or bless God if it has no effect and accomplishes nothing? Without any *quid pro quo* relation there is no point in believing in God. Job's wife is prepared to let go of such an ineffective relation with God. Her attitude seems fully understandable in the new situation, especially for the reader who witnessed the wager between God and Satan in heaven. However, Job does not agree with her. He does not sin with his lips. For seven days and seven nights he stays silent amongst the presence of his friends.

IV. Cursing the day of his birth

Job's reaction after seven days of silence strikes the reader in the face: he curses the day of his birth; he rebels and reveals himself in an unexpected manner. He who was so afraid that his sons might not have feared God enough and might have sinned now displays a conduct very different from and even contrary to the traditional view on piety and faith:[9]

Let the day perish in which I was born, and the night that said, 'A man-child is conceived.' Let that day be darkness! May God above not seek it, or light shine on it. Let gloom and deep darkness claim it. Let clouds settle upon it; let the blackness of the day terrify it. That night — let thick darkness seize it! Let it not rejoice among the days of the year; let it not come into the number of the months. Yes, let that night be barren; let no joyful cry be heard in it (3.3–7).

Job's complaint increases the tension that has been built up so far. The elaborate and intense lamentation shows that Job cannot accept the divine perspective of 'faith without a cause'. He is prepared to share his wife's point of view. What's the point in living if one is struck by misery for no reason? Instead of denying the existence of God he wants to end the relationship by denying his own existence. His life has to be erased by obliterating the day of his birth. The scenery of utter darkness and gloom depicts the impossibility for Job to live his life in a world *sine causa*. He is caught in a web of causality. There seems to be no other pattern of thinking at hand, or other point of view for understanding the world and his own place in it, if there is no reason for his suffering:

Why is light given to one in misery, and life to the bitter in soul, who long for death, but it does not come, and dig for it more than for hidden treasures; who rejoice exceedingly, and are glad when they find the grave? Why is light given to one who cannot see the way, whom God has fenced in? For my sighing comes like my bread, and my groanings are poured out like water. Truly the thing that I fear comes upon me, and what I dread befalls me. I am not at ease, nor am I quiet; I have no rest; but trouble comes (3.20–26).

The failure to understand God's way makes Job feel like a prisoner. Satan referred to God's fence of protection (1.10), Job sees only a fence of oppression. Job no longer desires to exist in a world of randomness. A relationship with God based on pure chance runs counter to all the conventions he knows and has lived by. The foundations for the meaning of life itself are swept away, since the logic of causality ceases to exist. It makes him depressed.

V. The divine perspective revisited

The images of God and man provided so far give rise to a lot of questions, especially with regard to the relationship between the heaven and the earth. Although God appraises certain forms of human conduct, this does not necessarily result in positive consequences for the human beings on earth. Even though causality rules God's behaviour in his relationship with Satan, this appears to be absent in his relationship with human beings. It turns out to be a matter of perspective, in which the perception of reality mainly depends on one's vantage point. The human characters involved have their own reasons for behaving in a certain manner, because each of them, be it Job, his wife, or his friends, acts according to his or her own views and interests. Their image of the world and their image of God is inevitably bound up with their place in that world.

At the same time the opening chapters of the book of Job pose a major dilemma. Without any reason for the course of humankind, it is difficult to understand God's position in the grand scheme of life. To have a 'faith without a cause' and to live a life in a 'framework *sine causa*' seem to imply that one lives in a world ruled by chance and arbitrariness. From a human point of view it means a life without any certainties, and as far as human conduct is concerned, anarchy and profligacy lie waiting. It is the kind of world-view Job complains about and cannot accept.

There is, however, another aspect of such a view. The conversation in heaven has shown that a reason is always a reason for someone, that causal relationships are related to vantage points and perspectives, and that therefore 'with or without a cause' is always related to someone, too. No one is able to share the divine perspective, confined as one is to limited perceptions. This does not imply that humankind is delivered over to the mercy of a God of randomness.[10] It docs mean, however, that from a human point of view we do not and cannot know all the reasons involved. People's positions on earth simply differ from God's position in heaven, and therefore his actions have a cause of their own.

Notes

1. This contribution presents the results of a cognitive linguistic approach to Job 1–3, i.e. the study of language based on how the world is experienced, perceived and conceptualized. For a general introduction to cognitive linguistics see F. Ungerer and H.-J. Schmid, *An Introduction to Cognitive Linguistics*, London and New York 1966; for a cognitive linguistic approach to the Hebrew Bible see A. H. Kamp, *Inner Worlds. A Cognitive Linguistic Approach of the Book of Jonah*, Biblical Interpretation Series Vol.68, Leiden 2004; also E. J. van Wolde (ed.), *Job 28. Cognition in Context*, Biblical Interpretation Series Vol.64, Leiden 1963.

2. The biblical quotations are taken from the New Revised Standard Version (1989), except for the translation of YHWH (in NRSV the LORD, here YHWH).

3. The Hebrew clause indicates a durative state of affairs that characterizes Job's

attitude in general. Cf. D. J. A. Clines, *Job 1–20*, Word Biblical Commentary 17, Waco, Texas 1989; W. Gesenius, E. Kautzsch and E. A. Cowley, *Gesenius' Hebrew Grammar*, Oxford ²1910, §112h.

4. See Clines, *Job* (n.3), p. xxxix.
5. Ibid., p. 15: 'Job's piety is scrupulous, even excessively so, if not actually neurotically anxious.'
6. For a more elaborate view on divine retribution, cf. E. J. van Wolde, 'Different Perspectives on Faith and Justice: The God of Jacob and the God of Job', *Concilium* 2002/1, pp. 17–23.
7. Cf. Y. Hoffman, *A Blemished Perfection. The Book of Job in Context*, Journal for the Study of the Old Testament Supplement Series 213, Sheffield 1996, p. 47; E. J. van Wolde, 'A Text-Semantic Study of the Hebrew Bible, illustrated with Noah and Job', *Journal of Biblical Literature* 113, 1994, pp. 19–35; Clines, *Job* (n.3), p. 16.
8. Cf. A. H. Kamp, 'World Building in Job 28: A Case of Conceptual Logic', in E. J. van Wolde (ed.), *Job 28. Cognition in Context* (n.1), pp. 307–19; J. Hartley, *The Book of Job*, New International Commentary on the Old Testament, Grand Rapids 1988, p. 67.
9. Cf. N. Habel, 'Earth First: Inverse Cosmology in Job', in id. and S. Wurst (eds), *The Earth Story in Wisdom Traditions*, Sheffield 2001, pp. 65–77.
10. A similar image of God occurs in the book of Jonah; see Kamp, *Inner Worlds* (n.1), pp. 223–34.

'But I, I would converse with the Almighty' (Job 13.3): Job and his Friends on God

PIERRE VAN HECKE

I. Introduction

The majority of the chapters of the book of Job are devoted to an increasingly hostile discussion between Job and the friends who came to visit him after he had been struck by disaster. After the prose introduction of chapters 1–2, sketching the narrative setting of the book, the dialogue between Job and his friends launches and develops the central problem with which the book is concerned and which the subsequent divine speeches and prose epilogue try to answer.

But what is that central problem? Since the friends decided to pay Job a consoling visit after they had heard about the calamities that had occurred to him, one could reasonably suppose that Job's suffering would be the main topic of the dialogue. But although this topic is not entirely absent from the discussion, it will be clear to anyone reading the dialogue attentively that it is not the central issue. Moreover, the divine answers both to Job (38–41) and to his friends (42.7–8) nowhere address the issue of Job's suffering, let alone that of human suffering in general.[1] It was Gerhard von Rad who insisted that it is not so much suffering that is problematical in the book of Job, but rather the credibility of God.[2] Indeed, Job and his friends fiercely discuss God's involvement in Job's suffering, and when God finally enters the discussion, he primarily reacts to what has been said about and to him in the course of the dialogue.

In the present article, I will therefore turn to the question of how God is spoken about and spoken to in the dialogue that forms the core of the book. A first hearing of the discussion will already make clear that the multiple voices do not perform in unison or in harmonic chords, but rather play in polyphonic counterpoint, with similar motifs recurring in the different voices, yet also at times jarring dissonances. Moreover, judging by the reaction of his divine critic, Job himself seems to perform at least two staves at the same time: God both rebukes Job for what he has said about him, defining Job's words as 'speaking without knowledge' (38.2), and, a few chapters later, indirectly commends Job for what he has said, in contrast to the friends (42.7).

In what respects do the voices of Job and his friends differ and in what do they agree? And what are the multiple voices within Job's own words, which prompt God to his double reaction? These are the questions to which I will now turn.

II. God as the cause of suffering

From his first reply to his friends on, Job is very clear about God's involvement in his suffering:

> For the arrows of the Almighty are in me;
> My spirit absorbs their poison;
> God's terrors are arrayed against me (6.4).[3]

In straightforward military and hunting metaphors, Job expresses his conviction that it is God himself who causes him to suffer. Although Job nowhere provides any arguments for this claim, it is repeated on different occasions in his replies (e.g., 7.14; 9.34; 19.6–12, 21 and particularly 16.9). Apparently Job considers it self-evident that God's hand is behind his suffering, witnessing to his (implicit) belief that all human suffering is the result of divine punishment for sins committed. When, in his first reply, Job turns from speaking to his friends to addressing God himself, he therefore asks why God does not forgive him for the sins he might have committed (7.17–21). In his first reaction, Job could not but explain his suffering as the result of God's chastisement. In this regard, Job does not differ from his friends. The latter keep repeating throughout their discussion with Job that God indeed punishes the wicked (e.g. 20.29). Moreover, Job and his friends also agree on the fact that this direct divine involvement is in accord with the rules of justice and righteousness.

Although Job and his friends share the same conceptual framework of divine retribution as the explanation for human suffering, their respective interpretations of Job's actual suffering is very different. For the friends, Job's suffering is a clear indicator of the fact that he has sinned. The longer they speak with Job, the more they are convinced of this view. Seeing the full extent of Job's suffering, they come to the inescapable conclusion: if Job is afflicted that much, it can only be because of his great sins, which God is now punishing (22.4–5). As mentioned above, Job agrees with his friends on God's right and duty to reward good behaviour and punish evil deeds.

However, slowly recovering from the numbing blows of disaster, Job tries to make sense of what has happened to him and concludes that the principle of divine retribution has failed to work in his case. Job knows that he is not wicked, at least not to the point of deserving the suffering that has overtaken him. Surprisingly, Job's conclusion about the failure of the retributive principle does not lead him to reject the principle as such. What has proven wrong in Job's own case is not the principle of retribution itself – which is righteous – but God's application of it: God has failed to act according to his own moral standards. To the friends, this idea is inadmissible: 'Will God pervert the right, will the Almighty pervert justice?', Bildad asks rhetorically (8.3). To Job, this conclusion is the only way of saving both the principle of retribution, which is the basis for any human moral order,[4] and his own innocence. At the end of the dialogue, Job cannot but conclude that God has deprived him of justice (27.2).

III. God's credibility

Obviously, the insight that God would be violating his own principles of justice seriously affects and troubles Job's idea of God. His reaction to this new fact is of psychologically realistic complexity. Like someone who has been cheated in a relation of strong mutual trust and affection, Job turns against his divine partner in disappointment and anger, but at the same time clings to this relationship and tries to save it. Rather than monolithically blaming God and refusing any further relationship, Job keeps returning to God, not only because, in his view, only God is able to restore his lot, but also because he is unable to give up his lifelong relationship with God. Apart from acerbic accusations and wry reproaches, Job's speeches also contain the most personal affirmation of God's creatorship to be found in the Hebrew Bible (10.8–12). In these verses, Job acknowledges God as his personal creator. As the context of these verses demonstrates, however, it is this intimate relationship with God, which Job is unable to give up and does not want to, that renders his affliction all the sharper. Job not only suffers *because of* God, but also suffers '*from* God':[5] more than anything else, Job suffers from the fact that he has become God's enemy – or so he supposes.[6] However hostile he believes God to have been to him, Job therefore keeps yearning – until the very end of the dialogue – for the day that their relation will be restored:

> I cry to you, but you do not answer me,
> I wait, but you do not consider me (31.20).

This is precisely the point on which Job's speaking about God differs fundamentally from that of the friends. If, as von Rad suggested, the central problem in the book of Job is that of the 'credibility of God', the friends limit this problem to the credibility of God as the guarantor of moral order, whereas for Job, not only God's credibility as warrantor of principles, but also his credibility as interlocutor and as relational partner is at stake. For that reason, their respective defences of God's credibility, too, are at variance with each other: the friends defend God's credibility by maintaining that the retributive principle has always been and still is operative, even if this implies condemning Job as a wicked sinner. Job, for his part, gives up God's credibility as the guarantor of the retributive principle, but tries to save his credibility as a partner by leaving open – and creating – possibilities for communication and relation, as will be shown below.

IV. Job's desire for relationship

Job's desire for maintaining the relationship with God finds its clearest expression in his repeated and outspoken resolution to speak with God, and indeed in the way he actually addresses God in the course of the dialogues. As has been observed by many commentators, the theme of 'speaking to God' is one of the central issues in Job's first replies in the dialogue. Moreover, it is the only theme that displays a clear thematic development throughout the dialogues, the other topics being treated in a recapitulatory and elaborative fashion, without thematic progression.[7] In the first of his replies (chapters 6–7), Job does not yet mention the possibility of having a conversation with God, although he does address God at the end of his reply, as we will see. In his opening reply, Job is still too busy recovering from the blows of suffering, wishing he were dead (6. 8–9), as in the complaint of chapter 3, but also formulating his first protest and resistance against what has happened to him. His second reply (chapters 9–10) marks a first decisive step: Job toys with the idea of talking out his differences with God and, more specifically, of engaging in a lawsuit with God. In this second reply, however, the idea of directly discussing with God is still considered an impossible hypothesis by Job. Job supposes that God would not answer him anyway (9.3), or, in the unlikely case that he would, that he would not really listen to his words (9.16). Moreover, Job is quite sure that he himself could not answer God, nor present his arguments to him if there were ever a trial between them (9.14). But in spite of his doubts about the outcome of his desire, he continues his plea for a confrontation with God, not only because this is the only way in which he could ever be vindicated, but also because it is the only way in which his relationship with God could be restored.

Job's strong determination to speak to God himself comes to a climax in his third reply (chapters 12–14), not coincidentally Job's first reply after he has heard each of his three friends. In this reply, Job addresses his friends more directly than ever before, trying to make clear in what respects he differs from his friends. First of all, he stresses that he is not inferior to his friends as far as knowledge and wisdom are concerned, and that he knows all the (traditional) arguments with which the friends defend the validity of the retributive principle and the credibility of God as its guarantor. The first two verses of chapter 13 formulate it as follows (compare also with 12.2–3):

> My eye has seen all this;
> My ear has heard and understood it.
> What you know, I know also;
> I am not less than you (13.1–2).

Job then goes on to show in what respect he and his friends *are* different: it is not knowledge, but the way in which they involve God in their respective speeches that sets them apart:

> But I, I would converse with the Almighty;[8]
>   I insist on arguing with God.
> But you invent lies;
>   All of you are quacks (13.3–4).

A few verses later, the lies of the friends are spelt out: the friends speak unjustly on God's behalf, they plead God's cause on his behalf (13.7), whereas Job desires to converse with God in an immediate and unmediated way, allowing God to speak for himself. Job's earlier doubts about the possibility of speaking to God have now made way for a dogged determination to engage in a conversation with God, come what may. Job's resolution to speak to God proves genuine when he formally files a lawsuit against God (13.18). Since Job feels wronged by God, he envisages his conversation with God as a legal confrontation. Throughout the dialogues it becomes clear, however, that what Job really desires is not a lawsuit as such, but an honest conversation. The lawsuit is merely the most suitable form in which Job believes this conversation could take place.[9] As the verbal form used in 13.18 (performative perfect) indicates, Job's declaration that he will litigate against God has performative force; i.e., by declaring it, the lawsuit is a fact. Therefore, the clause can best be read as: 'See, I hereby file a lawsuit.' This formal resolution is a decisive step and a point of no return both for Job and for God: the litigation cannot be undone and the parties involved will have to play their parts. Immediately after this resolution, Job asks God to determine the formal conditions under which the lawsuit will be held: Job asks God not to overpower him, but he leaves God the freedom either to ask his own questions or to answer Job's. Even though Job has given up on God's credibility as the guarantor of retributive justice, he insists on speaking with God – viz., in the context of a lawsuit – not only so that he could personally be vindicated, but also because in this way God could reaffirm his credibility as a communication partner, which is essential to Job.

V. Job speaks to God

Job's formal resolution to enter into a legal confrontation with God is actually the formalization and radicalization of what he had been doing throughout the dialogues, viz., addressing God. Both in his first and his second replies, Job turned from speaking to the friends to speaking to God (7.12–21; 10.2–22), and he also does so in the third and the fourth replies (13.20–14.22; 17.1–5). More than the content of Job's words, the sheer fact that he turns to God shows to what extent he values his direct relationship to God. Given this fact, one could wonder why Job insists so much on conversing with God (13.3), after having addressed God a number of times. Moreover, it is remarkable that after his formal resolution to converse with God, he barely addresses God any longer in the replies to his friends. The two points are related. What Job envisages in 13.3 is not only addressing God but having a conversation with him, i.e. conversing with God on equal terms.[10] This is not a regular thing to long for, since in the Hebrew Bible only very few people are said to have had a conversation with God (using the same Hebrew expression as in 13.3), viz., Abraham, Moses, Joshua and David.[11] After Job has formally asked for such a conversation, in the context of a lawsuit, he can only wait for God to enter this conversation, which he will eventually do, after 25 more chapters of waiting on Job's side. During this divine silence, Job frequently repeats his desire to speak with God (e.g. 23.3–6; 31.35), but he does not address God again. Instead, he turns to oaths, putting his own existence at risk and showing, once again, 'that his deepest desire is to have a genuine relationship with God for its own sake'.[12] Job's behaviour in the dialogues thus illustrates that his resolution to converse with God is genuine, as is his desire for a restored relation with God. Moreover, the course of the dialogues confirms that Job and his friends indeed differ fundamentally in the way they involve God in their speeches:

whereas Job addresses God in each of his first four replies and only stops
doing so for the reasons mentioned above, the friends do not speak a single
word to God, but do speak much about him and on his behalf. One could
object that it is precisely one of the friends, viz., Eliphaz, who first suggested
to Job that he would turn to God:

> But I would resort to God;
> I would lay my case before God (5.8).

This advice is given to Job even before he explicitly addressed God for the
first time. Moreover, the recommendation to turn to God is repeated a
number of times in the friends' later speeches (8.5; 11.13; 22.27). After all,
then, the friends do not seem that different from Job as far as their speaking
to God is concerned. But there is more to it. As commentators have
remarked, the friends' suggestion to Job is strongly religious: they recom-
mend him to engage in religious practices as a means of reordering his life,
as a way out of turmoil.[13] These practices involve repentance and the
acknowledgment that praise is becoming for God. While their advice is well-
intentioned, it disregards Job's needs. Religious practices and prayer can
have their reordering effects only if the credibility of the divine addressee is
beyond doubt. Job's present relationship to God, and his understanding of
how God apparently relates to him, do not allow him to surrender to the religious practices his friends propose. In his context, repairing his damaged
relation with God and allowing God to prove his credibility take priority
over the language of praise. And it must be repeated: the friends' repeated
suggestion to turn to God has not inspired them actually to approach God in
prayer nor to help Job in doing so, while Job's desire to converse with God is
not limited to words and eventually even elicits an answer from God, albeit
not the answer he expected.

VI. God speaks to Job

Job's vision of God in the dialogues is complex, but psychologically realistic:
on the one hand, Job regards God as the cause of all his suffering, failing to
apply the just rules of retribution, and, on the other, he sees him as a lost
partner or interlocutor with whom he wishes to talk out the differences they
have.[14] This complex vision calls for a complex answer from God. After
Job's relentless and determined requests, the fact that God finally agrees to
enter into the discussion comes as a relief. As a matter of fact, the formulaic
introductions of God's answers (38.1; 40.1,6) make clear that God is the first

one really to answer Job. Whereas the replies of the friends are invariably and stereotypically introduced with the phrase 'X answered and said,' God's answers explicitly mention the name of his interlocutor: 'God answered *Job* and said.' Job's desire for conversing with God is thus granted. In his answer, which is the topic of a different article in the present issue, God immediately makes clear, however, that Job was incorrect in calling him to account for not applying retributive justice. After this reproof, however, God turns to the friends and blames them for not having spoken as Job has done (42.7). Since the expression used in this verse is exactly the same as in the crucial verse 13.3 ('converse with God'), it seems more than likely that God commends the fact that Job was willing to engage in a conversation with him, rather than to speak about him or on his behalf, as the friends have done.[15] Apparently, Job's determination to discuss with God, even when it took the form of a litigation, is more valued than the friends' vigorous defence of his credibility as guarantor of moral order. Job's partly mistaken view at least left God the opportunity to demonstrate his credibility – and his alterity – *as God*.

Notes

1. See D. J. A. Clines, 'Does the Book of Job Suggest that Suffering is Not a Problem?', in D. J. A. Clines, H. Lichtenberger and H.-P. Müller (eds), *Weisheit in Israel. Beitrage des Symposiums "Das Alte Testament und die Kultur der Moderne" anlasslich des 100. Geburtstags Gerhard von Rads (1901–1971) Heidelberg 18–21 Oktober 2001*, Altes Testament und Moderne 12, Münster 2003.

2. G. von Rad, *Weisheit in Israel*, Neukirchen-Vluyn 1970, p. 286 (ET *Wisdom in Israel*, London 1972).

3. The biblical quotations are taken from the JPS translation (*Jewish Publication Society Hebrew-English Tanakh*, The Jewish Publication Society, Philadelphia 1999·5759).

4. See von Rad, *Weisheit in Israel* (n.2), p. 173.

5. See F. Mies, 'Le livre de Job. De l'excès du mal à l'altérité du mal?', *NReTh* 121, 1999, pp. 177–96 : 192–194, inspired by Karl Barth's interpretation of the book of Job.

6. D. J. A. Clines, *Job 1–20*, Word Biblical Commentary 17, Dallas 1989, p. 171.

7. Ibid., p. 377.

8. I have modified the JPS translation of 13.3a in order to bring out the parallel opening of vv. 3 and 4 in the Hebrew text and in order to reflect my interpretation of the verb given below.

9. See C. A. Newsom, *The Book of Job. A Contest of Moral Imaginations*, Oxford 2003, pp. 150–61.

10. See *Theological Dictionary of the Old Testament* II, pp. 105–6.
11. See P. van Hecke, 'From Conversation about God to Conversation with God. The Case of Job', in J. Haers and P. De Mey (eds), *Theology and Conversation: Towards a Relational Theology*, BETL 172, Leuven 2004, pp. 115–124: 121.
12. J. E. Hartley, 'From Lament to Oath. A Study of Progression in the Speeches of Job', in W. A. M. Beuken (ed.), *The Book of Job*, BEThL 114, Leuven 1994, pp. 79–100: 88.
13. Newsom, *The Book of Job* (n.9), pp. 105–15.
14. See also J. L. Crenshaw, 'The Concept of God in Old Testament Wisdom', in L. G. Perdue, B. B. Scott and W.J. Wiseman (eds), *In Search of Wisdom. Essays in Memory of John G. Gammie*, Louisville, KY 1993, pp. 1–18: 12.
15. See P. van Hecke, 'From Conversation about God to Conversation with God. The Case of Job' (n. 11), *passim*.

The Verdict on/of God at the End of Job

NORMAN C. HABEL

The ending of Job has long been a hot exegetical topic, whether that ending be read as the final five chapters (38–42) or simply the final chapter (42). In either case, the final chapter incorporates a closing verdict on God both in the words from Job (42.1–6) and in God's own words from the mouth of the narrator (42.7–9). Each of these verdicts is, I believe, linked to the legal metaphor fundamental to the structure of Job.

The irony and ambiguity of the final words of Job (42.1–6) have led to a plethora of interpretations).[1] These include:

- Job completely surrenders to the will of God, repents of his arrogant attitude and stands humble before his God.
- Job is reconciled to God, coming to an understanding of God's governance of creation and is once more a wise one who fears God.
- Job's words reflect a comic irony. God's bravado from the whirlwind reflects God's attempt to handle Job's exposing of God's inconsistency. Job mollifies God with his 'tongue in cheek' confession.
- Job's speech is his final act of defiance. While Job recognizes his human limitations, he rejects a deity who answers human cries of despair with arrogant boastings from a tempest.

If, in the light of current research, we recognize afresh the legal framework of Job, the final speech of Job (42.2–6) amounts not only to a summation of Job before he leaves the court, but to an indirect verdict on God by Job, the human litigant. A close reading of each line of that speech is therefore warranted. I render Job's summation as follows:

I know that you can do everything
And that no scheme of yours can be thwarted.
(You said,)
'Who is this that obscures my design without knowledge?'
Indeed I have spoken without discernment

Of things beyond me which I do not know.
(You said,)
'Hear now and I will speak,
I will ask and you will inform me.'
I have heard you with my ears,
But now my eyes have seen you.
Therefore I retract
And repent of dust and ashes (42.2–6).

I. A God with intimidating power

In the preceding context, the powerful speeches of God from the tempest deserve to be recognized as more than argumentation designed to convince an uninformed human. They also serve to intimidate the litigant, to bring Job to his knees and force him to withdraw his accusations or settle. How dare a mere mortal challenge a deity before whom the great Leviathan surrenders? 'Have you an arm like God's? Can you thunder with a voice like his?' (40.9).

Job, of course, has long been aware of God's standover tactics and does not buckle beneath this new pressure.

If I summoned him to court and he answered,
I do not believe he would hear my voice.
He would crush me with a whirlwind
And increase my wounds without cause.
He would not let me catch my breath,
But would sate me with bitterness.
If it be a trial of strength—he is the mighty One!
If it be a trial at court—who will arraign him for me? (9.16–19).

When God does appear in a whirlwind and attempts to crush Job, Job stands his ground. After God's first barrage of heavy questions, Job admits that he is small but adds,

I have spoken once, I will not answer.
Twice, and will do so no more (40.5).

Job has stated his case against God and will not attempt to respond to God's claims as though Job were now the accused and obliged to 'answer' in court. The expression 'x or x + 1' is an idiom that in law indicates completeness.[2]

Job has stated his case and it still stands. What God has said does not challenge Job's claim of innocence. Job refuses to be intimidated. So God increases the intimidation pressure on Job and proceeds to confront Job with another expression of divine power — the control of Behemoth and Leviathan. After God's second defence and challenge, Job responds with the famous words of his summation, each line of which deserves, I believe, close scrutiny (42.2–6).

The opening lines (42.2) of Job's summation are a response to God's power tactics. Job's indirect verdict is that God plays devious power games. God, as God, can do anything. The negative innuendo in this assertion is that God has 'schemes' like the one revealed in the initial scene before the heavenly court (1.6–12). God had challenged Job's understanding of God's design (*'etsa*) of the cosmos (38.2). Job subverts this challenge by declaring that God has schemes (*mezimma*), a term that implies devious ways and means (21.27; Prov. 12.2). Job is not praising God for his power but indirectly continuing his challenge to the way God runs the world. Job's verdict on God the scheming spy still stands (cf. ch. 7). Job later admits that he does not know everything about the mysteries of the cosmos, but he does 'know' one thing: God is a powerful force. Job has experienced that power in his life and observed God's destructive ways in nature (12.13–15). Job knows the God of power as a God of chaos and senseless destruction. He does not retract this accusation.

God's intimidating power is not only evident in nature or society, it is also something Job has experienced personally. The language of God's relentless attack on Job illustrates just how forcefully Job has experienced this oppressive divine power:

> El delivers me over to the evil
> And hurls me into the hands of the wicked.
> I was at ease, but he smashed and smashed me;
> Seized my neck, then bashed and bashed me.
> He set me up as his target;
> His archers surrounded me.
> He pierced my kidneys without mercy;
> He spilled my bile on the ground.
> He breached me breach after breach;
> He charged me like a warrior (16.11–13).

The opening lines in Job's final speech (42.2) reiterate that God is all-powerful and that no 'scheme' can be thwarted, whether it be to turn creation into chaos or to attack a human being with the military might of a celestial warrior.

II. A God with superior wisdom

In God's opening speech, God sought to turn the tables, put Job on trial and force him to 'answer' (*'ana*). God challenged Job, as the one who has a lawsuit against Shaddai, to 'answer' God (40.2). In his response to God's initial challenge, Job refuses to 'answer' as a legal adversary (40.5). In his summation, however, Job does respond, briefly and to the point. He quotes God twice to make his position clear (42.3–4). The first quotation reads:

Who is this who obscures my design without knowledge? (42.3).

In this abbreviation of God's original challenge to Job (38.2–3), God claims that Job lacks the knowledge or wisdom to comprehend God's design and cosmic purpose (*'etsa*). The focus has moved from God's power, something that Job knows all too well, to God's wisdom as the cosmic designer. In God's opening challenge, God introduces the mystery of how Earth is secured on its foundations (38.4–7). God explicitly challenges Job's discernment (*bina*), his intellectual capacity as one of the wise (38.4). The verb *bin* is a technical term in wisdom literature referring to the cognitive skills of a wise person as he/she seeks to analyse and distinguish a phenomenon in nature or society.[3]

In response to this challenge from God, Job responds that he lacks the necessary wisdom or discernment (*bina*) to comprehend the mysteries of the cosmos. This concession, however, is not a problem for Job. He has never claimed the wisdom to comprehend the design of the cosmos. In God's speech, God took Job on a tour of the universe and confronted him with the distinctive way, code or law that governs each of its major physical components — the sea, Earth, the deep, lightning, the skies (38.4–38). The final challenge on this tour is whether Job can comprehend the wisdom within the clouds, the inner code or way that determines their nature and movement (38.36–38). All parts of nature, like the clouds, have their inner wisdom or laws that govern their operation.[4] And Job has no problem admitting that he lacks the cognitive capacity to probe these mysterious laws of nature. That is not the issue. The problem is that God has arbitrarily harassed and abused an innocent human being.

The unwritten implication of this admission, however, is that a God who possesses superior wisdom about how the universe functions, the 'way' of things in the cosmos, ought to understand the 'way' of humans and act with corresponding wisdom.

III. A God with elusive justice

Job's second quotation from God's speeches comes as somewhat of a surprise, taking us back to the basic issue of who is taking whom to court. Job had challenged God to answer the charges of injustice perpetrated on an innocent human being, demanding that God appear as an adversary in court (31.35). God's response is to try to silence Job as the accuser and to demand instead that Job answers God's challenges:

> Hear now and I will speak,
> I will ask and you will inform me (42.4).

The verb rendered 'inform' is more precisely 'cause me to know'. There is an ironic play on the verb 'to know' throughout this speech. Job claims to 'know' about God's intimidating power, but does not make a similar claim to 'know' about the mysteries of wisdom. Now God is demanding that Job answer and impart 'knowledge' to God.

We are then confronted by the third assertion in Job's summation, a word that initially seems relatively clear, but upon reflection confronts us with a major enigma. Literally the verse reads:

> With the hearing of my ears I have heard/hear you.
> And now with my eyes I have seen/see you (42.5).

In a recent article, a fellow Australian, Antony Campbell,[5] focussed especially on this verse as the key to reading Job's final speech. He quite rightly challenged my interpretation of this text in my commentary.[6] I implied that the advent of God in the whirlwind to confront God in court was equivalent to a theophany. Not only did Job hear, but he also 'saw' God in the form of the whirlwind. That appearance of God in court vindicated Job.

My reading may still be correct, but as Campbell points out, there is no explicit statement that Job saw anything visually.[7] Job heard God speak from the whirlwind, but nothing is said of Job actually seeing God. What then is the significance of Job's claim that he 'sees' God? Campbell's solution is to maintain that Job must see God 'outside the text'. He writes,

> Because the 'seeing' is not in the text, it is a legitimate possibility to
> assume that the reference is to activity outside the text, to something of

the experience of life. The text has been about words—from Job, the friends, Elihu and God. To move beyond these words ('and now'), it may be necessary to look to a way of knowing without words.[8]

Job's reply is in response to God's challenge for Job to take the stand and answer God as his accuser. Job ignores the challenge and makes a counter claim. Essentially Job says, in the first line of his response, 'I have heard you, God. That's it. There is no more to say. There is no explicit case against me.'

Why does Job follow with a second line about claiming to 'see' God? How does that claim complement Job's responses so far? Is his 'seeing' necessarily 'outside the text'?

A close study of the verb 'to see' (*ra'a*) in the book of Job and the wider wisdom context reveals a number of relevant meanings. The verb sometimes refers to a physical sighting like 'seeing the eyelids of dawn' (3.9). More frequently, however, it means to recognize and testify to something that is part of human experience, such as 'seeing the good' (7.7; 9.25), 'seeing anguish' (2.13), 'seeing tragedy' (6.21) or 'seeing a downfall' (21.20).

The verb is also used in wisdom literature to refer to an aspect of the cognitive process and, in that process, is linked with the verb *bin*, to distinguish, discern, analyse and hence come to know.[9] The pairing of these two verbs also happens in Job (9.11; 11.11; 28.23–24). Hearing and seeing can also be linked as evidence of understanding something (13.1). In some texts, the verb to see (*ra'a*) seems to stand as shorthand for the total cognitive process (Prov. 6.7).

When Job claims to have 'seen' God, therefore, the focus is not necessarily on an actual sighting but more likely on Job's claim to have finally discerned God's presence, to have experienced God in such a way as to claim that cognitively he 'knows' that God was there. God has confronted Job with a demand to 'answer' and for Job that experience is evidence of God's presence.

To appreciate the significance of Job's claim that he has finally discerned God's presence, we need to remember the frequent frustration of Job as he sought to find ways to induce this elusive God to come out of hiding, cease celestial harassment and confront Job in court. Job accused God of being an elusive spy who tests humans relentlessly but never shows his face (7.7–8, 17–20). Job complained that he had no one who could arraign God, bring God out of hiding, put one hand on God's shoulder and one hand on Job's and force God to face his victim in court (9.19, 32–35).

Nowhere is Job's frustration with his elusive adversary more evident than in chapter 23: Job's great desire is to locate God, enter his dwelling if necessary, and finally 'press my suit to his face' (23.4). The intent is clear: Job wants a face-to-face encounter with God in court. This frustration is apparent as Job cries:

> Behold, if I go East—he is not there!
> West—I do not discern (*bin*) him!
> North—in his concealment I cannot behold him!
> South—he is hidden and I cannot see (*ra'a*) him! (23.8–9).

This elusive hidden deity knows the 'way' of Job, but Job cannot locate God, cannot meet him face to face. His legal challenge for God to appear in court is Job's final tactic (31.35–37). And it works. Job is actually confronted with God's legal demand to 'answer' (3.3; 40.2; 42.4). God has 'appeared' in court, whether that corresponds to a theophanic sighting or some other experience of God's accusing presence. Job discerns God's presence in God's accusations from the whirlwind. In so doing he 'sees' God; he has forced his elusive opponent to leave his hiding place and 'appear' in court. Job has achieved his goal and forced his hidden God to show his 'face'.

IV. A God without a case

The final — and perhaps the most infamous — line of Job's summation has been variously translated. I am still convinced by the evidence that the implied object of the two verbs is probably 'dust and ashes', the symbol of Job's case and status as a litigant. Here Job declares his intention to leave the court, to abandon the case. The most likely translation then is:

> Therefore I despise/retract
> And repent of dust and ashes (42.6).

Campbell characterizes this verse as Job's 'exit line'.[10] But what a line! God enters the court and Job exits! Job has finally managed to get God into court only to be abandoned by his human adversary. God, as it were, tastes some of his own medicine.

'Dust and ashes' seem to represent Job as an alienated sufferer and litigant before God. Job initially separated himself from his community by sitting in 'ashes' (2.8) and his friends expressed sympathy by throwing 'dust' in the air (2.12). 'Dust and ashes' also seems to connote the self-negation and humiliation Job experiences as the object of God's abuse (30.19). For Job, being in 'dust and ashes' means being the public victim and more than a 'symbol of being mute and submissive before God'.[11]

He now repudiates that victim status. He chooses no longer to assume the role of victim, litigant or adversary. He is leaving the court with his head held high, having 'seen' God. The implication of this dramatic exit is that Job believes he is vindicated. Job is neither rebellious nor arrogant — he leaves as a man of integrity with nothing more to say.

In spite of God's efforts to confront Job with demands that he 'answer', God's accusations have not addressed Job's claim. God may have challenged Job's power and wisdom, but they have not seriously challenged his integrity. All that God achieves through his speeches is to reveal that Job's knowledge of the design of the cosmos is inferior to that of God. God presents no real case against Job, no serious accusation of blasphemy, hybris or wrongdoing. Job remains innocent of any charges and God has not successfully defended himself against Job's accusations. God has no case. Job walks free.

In the frame narrative at the beginning of the book, Job's integrity is recognized before the court of heaven, in spite of all the physical disasters that befall him. Now, after 40 chapters that include spiritual harassment by God, emotional turmoil caused by friends and the inner anguish of pursuing a case against God, Job's integrity is still not shaken. Job leaves the court with his head held high and, as it were, shakes the dust off his feet.

V. A God with a measure of justice

When Job leaves the court and God's challenge is left hanging, God could well have retaliated with an appropriate form of punishment for alleged defiance and disrespect of the Almighty. No such retaliation is forthcoming. Perhaps we could have anticipated a verdict from God, whether in or out of court, that Job was indeed innocent and that Job's integrity had not been violated. We could even imagine this hounding, harassing and hard-headed deity finally showing a little compassion and saying 'Sorry!'. After all, God was the party who was ultimately responsible for putting Job through his ordeal. And God had hit Job with a barrage of challenges that avoided Job's accusation of divine complicity in Job's experience of injustice. There is, however, no apparent indication of comfort or compassion on God's part.

God's response (42.7–8) to Job's summation is equivalent to an out-of-court settlement. God, however, does not even have the decency to speak to Job personally and assure him of his innocence. Instead, we meet a frustrated God who is ready to take out his anger on Job's friends. 'My anger has flared up against you,' says God. It seems that because God could not rattle Job, God turns on the friends and threatens them for not speaking the truth.

That verdict seems a little harsh. After all, the friends had taken God's side and sought to present God's version of the truth as they had learned it from tradition. They were not devious. Yet God now turns on his supporters and demands a sacrifice to expiate their guilt. To add insult to injury, the friends are required to ask Job to act as mediator and perform the sacrifice on their behalf. The victim who longed for a mediator to handle his case with God is now required by God to be the mediator for the friends who were his accusers. As mediator before God, Job is no longer a litigant. Job's integrity is recognized.

There is, of course, a measure of justice in this out-of-court settlement! Job overhears God saying that the friends have not spoken 'the truth about me as did my servant Job' (42.7). The term truth (*nekona*) refers to that which is proven correct (Deut. 17.4). God admits that Job is innocent, that he has spoken the truth about God, presumably also in Job's final speech — his summation about God's power, wisdom and elusive presence as an adversary at court.

God's angry words to the friends include a backhanded declaration of Job's innocence, an out-of-court settlement in which God avoids (a) employing the formula for an *in personam* verdict to the winning party 'you are in the right' (*tsaddiq 'atta*, Prov. 24.24)[12] and (b) any corresponding public verdict that God was, in fact, in the wrong.

There is also a measure of justice when God 'restores Job's fortunes' (42.10). The rendering 'restore' (*shub*) may be fortuitous and suggest 'restorative justice' rather than 'retributive justice'. Throughout the book of Job the friends espoused the classical doctrine of retribution and reward — the guilty are punished with appropriate disasters and the faithful are rewarded with blessings. Job's life is a total repudiation of that doctrine. It would seem preferable, therefore, to read Job's reversal of fortunes as a divine restoration rather than as a reward for speaking the truth, showing a measure of justice rather than rewarding integrity (42.8). To restore 'double' is a recognised biblical tradition (Ex. 22.3, 6, 8). Presumably this restoration includes healing the wounds inflicted by God (cf. 5.8), but no such healing is reported.

While there may have been a measure of justice, there is no compassion and no comfort forthcoming from God. Job's God may be all-powerful, exceedingly wise and ready, when pushed to the edge, to expose his presence, but this deity nowhere shows any mercy or kindness towards Job, even though God is willing to call him 'my servant' at the end as he did at the very beginning (1.8; 42.7).

A number of scholars suggest that God's love and mercy are implied in the speeches from the whirlwind. B. Lynne Newell, for example, proposes that 'as a result of Yahweh's second speech Job realized that he did not understand God's mercy in judgement'.[13] Gutiérrez goes so far as to say that the ending of Job is about God's love reaching beyond justice.[14] However, neither the speeches about Behemoth and Leviathan nor the portrait of God's rule over creation make any specific connection with God's mercy, love or compassion for humans.

The only compassion for Job comes from relatives and former acquaintances, not from God or the three so-called friends (42.11). Job's family and acquaintances are willing to eat with Job in his house, a mark of acceptance back into normal life and community. More significantly, however, they are ready to 'console and comfort' Job. The critical point in this process is that they all concur with the narrator's verdict on God: God has been the source of the 'evil' that Job has suffered.

Job thereby receives a second indirect verdict: Job is innocent and God is guilty of perpetrating evil. There is also a measure of justice here in that God's part in the plot is exposed for all to see.

VI. The God at the end

We might expect that because the frame narrative of Job has a so-called 'happy ending' the final image of God may also be revised to make God more kind and loving. Instead, the portrait of God at the end of Job remains complex and ambiguous. The power of a deity who can handle Leviathan with ease remains unchallenged. Job, however, does not retract his earlier assertions that God uses his power to effect chaos on Earth and in society (12.13–25). God's opening speech (ch. 38) may provide an indirect defence of God's cosmic power, but God's words never answer the specific charges of Job. Job also claims that God uses his power unjustly to harass and hound innocent humans like Job (16.6–17). God does not choose to answer that charge because God is clearly vulnerable.

The wisdom of God as the great designer of the cosmos is not challenged by Job. Job acknowledges that the ways and laws that govern the universe are incomprehensible to him. God, however, is faced with the reality that Job too has a 'way' that delineates his purpose in life. At the very beginning of his cries of anguish he screams,

> Why does God give light to the sufferer,
> Life to the bitter in spirit…
> Why, to a person whose way (*derek*) is hid,
> Hedged around by Eloah? (3.20–23).

The wisdom of God may guide the 'ways' of the cosmos, ensuring that they function according to their inner purpose. However, no such wisdom guides the way God treats mortals in misery. The God of wisdom may reflect a superior mind but it seems devoid of compassion. And as Campbell makes clear, the question of why this wise deity hides the 'way' of a person in misery is never answered.[15]

This wise and all-powerful God also claims to be a God of justice, but that justice seems to be as elusive as the God Job is seeking to locate. Job would not be seeking to summon God to court if he did not think that there was a possibility of justice. By God remaining distant, hidden, elusive and abusive, Job appears to all the world to be the guilty party not the innocent victim. When God challenges Job in court, Job may perceive a glimmer of justice. God has at least finally appeared and demanded Job 'answer' the Almighty. God, however, continues to put Job to the test. He seeks to turn the tables and make Job answer God's demands. In the end, these demands are empty and God has no case. The elusive God has appeared; Job has 'seen' God and that is enough. Job is free and God has lost the case!

The only justice Job can savour is the indirect verdict reflected in God's words to the friends and the comfort of relatives and acquaintances for the 'evil' God has inflicted on Job. There is no hint of God's compassion or mercy. The verdict of God at the end of Job is, in turn, a verdict on God — a God of power, wisdom and elusive justice, but without compassion.

Notes

1. Norman C. Habel, *The Book of Job: A Commentary*, London and Philadelphia 1985, p. 577.
2. Andrew Steinmann, 'The Graded Numerical Sayings in Job', in A. B. Beck and others (eds), *Fortunate Eyes that See: Essays in Honor of David Noel Freedman in Celebration of his Seventieth Birthday*, Grand Rapids 1995, pp. 288–97: 297.
3. Norman C. Habel, 'The Implications of God Discovering Wisdom in Earth', in Ellen van Wolde (ed.), *Job 28: Cognition in Context*, Leiden 2003, pp. 281–98: 284.
4. Ibid.
5. Anthony Campbell, 'The Book of Job: Two Questions, One Answer', *Australian Biblical Review* 51, 2003, pp. 15–25.
6. Habel, *Book of Job* (n.1), p. 582.
7. Campbell, 'The Book of Job' (n.5), p. 20.
8. Ibid., p. 21.
9. Habel, 'The Implications of God' (n.3), pp. 282–5.
10. Campbell, 'The Book of Job' (n.5), p. 20.

11. Samuel Balentine, '"What are Human Beings that You Make so Much of Them?" Divine Disclosure from the Whirlwind: "Look at Behemoth"', in Tod Linefelt and Timothy Beal (eds), *God in the Fray. A Tribute to Walter Brueggemann*, Minneapolis 1998, pp. 259–78: 277.

12. R. Westbrook, 'Biblical Law', in N. S. Hecht (ed.), *An Introduction to the History and Sources of Jewish Law*, Oxford 1996, pp. 1–17: 10.

13. B. Lynne Newell, 'Job: Repentant or Rebellious?', in Roy B. Zuck, *Sitting with Job. Selected Studies on the Book of Job*, Grand Rapids 1992, pp. 441–61.

14. Gustavo Gutiérrez, *On Job. God Talk and the Suffering of the Innocent*, Maryknoll, NY 1985, p 87.

15. Campbell, 'The Book of Job' (n.5), p. 25.

Job's God

DAVID J.A. CLINES

The Book of Job is a hymn to the inscrutability of God. Unlike some religions in which the deity is unknowable or virtually so, in the Book of Job it is not that nothing about God can be known; it is rather that too much about God is known, or at least may be said, for us to be sure that any statement we make about him is right or wrong. Is he a cosmic deity, far removed from the concerns of humans, or is he intimately involved with the lives and destinies of individual humans? Is he a compassionate god or a cruel monster? Does he govern the world according to the dictates of justice, or is he negligent of human affairs? All these positions are affirmed by the Book of Job, or at least by one of the speakers within its dialogues.

All the voices within the book contradict the others, so whom are we to believe? The friends, who speak as theologians representative of traditional and orthodox Hebrew piety? Job himself, who hurls accusations against God from the midst of dreadful suffering, and is perhaps not in his right mind? God, who steadfastly refuses to address the key questions that Job and the book have been raising? Or the author of the book and his spokesman the narrator, who take for themselves the last word that unsettles all that has previously been spoken?

Or is it perhaps not a matter of privileging one voice over another, of declaring Job in the right and the friends in the wrong, or God in the right and the author in the wrong, and so on, but of recognizing all the voices as the stuff of serious thinking about God, each with its perception, however partial, of an aspect of the divine reality, but none comprehensive, none beyond contradiction or dispute? We would of course like to find a resolution to the problems of the book, but perhaps a resolution is too much to hope for. If the book itself does not speak unequivocally, perhaps all we should attempt is to give an open yet critical hearing to all the voices in their manifoldness and dissonance.

That would be a tempting approach. But the Book of Job is not the report of a seminar in which all voices are equal. In its structure and texture, it invites a hierarchical positioning of the participants, according to which the voice of the friends is to be heard as the least credible, for in the epilogue God says that they have not spoken of him what is right (42.7–8). Job, at the same place, is said to have spoken what is right, and yet he is the object of the most severe criticism from God, and we readers know from the prologue that he is in any case under a terrible misapprehension about God's attitude toward him. It becomes hard to know whether his voice deserves more attention than that of the friends. We might have thought that the voice of God from the tempest (chs 38–41) would automatically command the submission of all readers of the book, and yet what Yahweh says there proves profoundly unsatisfactory to many readers, and the narrative of the book, in the epilogue, seems to ignore and undermine the thrust of the divine speeches. So in the end it is far from clear that one voice, and one voice alone, should be attended to; and in any case, the poet has set before us the utterances of all the interlocutors for our instruction and delectation, and we may do well to savour, in all its variety, their conflicted talk about God.

I. The voice of Job's three friends

Together, the three friends of Job, Eliphaz, Bildad and Zophar represent the traditional theology of Israel, a theology that Job himself also has adhered to until recent days. This is not a theology that celebrates the God of salvation, acting mightily for Israel at the exodus and at the conquest of the land, but an older, more fundamental theology that sees God as the designer and executor of a system of cosmic justice. According to this retributionary view of God, especially on the plane of the human individual, though also on the level of the nation, those who act properly are rewarded with blessings, while wrongdoers are punished. For Eliphaz and his friends, effecting that system of reward and punishment is God's primary activity as far as humans are concerned.

As for whether Job belongs with the righteous or the wicked, the friends differ among themselves; but they are at one in believing that he is being punished in some degree by God for his wrongdoing, and that his future hangs solely upon a change in his own behaviour. Eliphaz (Job 4–5; 15; 22) is clear about the reality of God as retributor:

> Recall now: What innocent man ever perished?
>   Where were the upright ever annihilated?
> As my experience goes, those who plant iniquity
>   and those who sow mischief reap due harvest.
> By a breath from God they perish (4.7–9).

But that is not bad news for Job, for he is among the righteous, and what he is suffering now is not fatal retribution like the wicked, but 'discipline' by way of reproof for minor misdemeanours, all kindly meant:

> Consider! Happy is the man whom God reproves!
>   So do not spurn the discipline of the Almighty.
> For he may wound, but he binds up the sore;
>   he may smite, but his hands heal (5.17–18).

Bildad (Job 8; 18; 25.1; 26.2–4; 25.2–6; 26.5–14) too knows God as the one who ensures exact retribution in the world of humans. When he says,

> Can God pervert justice?
>   Can the Almighty pervert what is right? (8.3),

we know he is thinking of the law of retribution, for he goes on to argue that the death of Job's children is all the evidence needed that they must have sinned greatly:

> Your sons sinned against him,
>   so he abandoned them to the power of their own guilt (8.4).

Job, on the other hand, is not dead; so his fault, whatever it is, does not appear to be fatal, and he may reasonably expect a happier future:

> Behold, God will not reject a blameless man,
>   nor will he uphold the evil-doer.
> He will yet again fill your mouth with laughter;
>   shouts of joy will be on your lips (8.20–21).

Zophar (Job 11; 20; 27.1, 7–10, 13–17; 24.18–24; 27.18–23), the most severe of the three friends, accepts the same principle, though he has his own estimation of the degree of Job's wrongdoing. It is not that Job's continued existence is proof that he has not sinned greatly, for, if the truth were to be told, Job no doubt deserves much more than he is suffering:

> But if only God would speak
>   Then you would know that God overlooks part of your sin (11.5–6).

Quite why God should 'overlook' some of Job's sin is hard to discern; no word is said of mercy, and it can hardly be that God does not pay enough attention to know what Job is truly culpable of. It is enough to know that there are 'mysteries' in the divine working (11.6) – which is to say, Zophar cannot himself explain how his belief in Job's greater sinfulness squares with his underlying principle of exact retribution. Nevertheless, he too thinks Job cannot be worthy of death, like the wicked; he too offers Job a positive view of the future, if only he will abandon his sin:

> If there is wrongdoing in your hand, renounce it
> then you will lift up your face, free of fault.
> You will forget your suffering,
>   remember it only as water that has flowed past.
> Then your life will be brighter than the noonday;
>   its darkness will be as morning light (11.14, 15–17).

Now it is very easy to mock the friends' concept of God as the executor of retribution, and to point to the myriad of examples we all know in which reward has been denied the godly and the wicked have escaped punishment. Yet the alternatives to this theology may be worse still: imagine a world in which there is simply no predictable correspondence between act and consequence. How will any parent inculcate right behaviour in children, how will any state warn the criminally inclined, if there is no underlying principle of retribution? The attractiveness of the theology is that it is not purely experiential and anecdotal, an accumulation of instances, but a systematic, principled thinking through of the way the world ought to work, should be governed, must be conceived. It posits a fundamental justice at the heart of God's design for the universe. From this perspective, any number of examples, or apparent examples, where it fails to be implemented cannot subvert the principle, for – although it is often stated as an account of what actually happens in the real world – it is not so much a description of reality as a blueprint for it.

It is, nonetheless, a very constrictive picture of God that emerges from the speeches of the three friends. To regard God as essentially the architect and sustainer of such a principle is a spare and somewhat impersonal theology. True, the friends are aware of some other aspects in the divine nature, the perfection of his knowledge, for example (11.7–9), his great wonders in nature (5.9–10), his works in creation (26.7–13), his healing hands (11.18), his pleasure in the innocent (22.23–29). But theirs is no rounded theology, and it will be for others in the book to broaden the scope of a depiction of God.

II. The voice of Elihu (Job 32–37; 28)

The fourth friend, Elihu the interloper, has no fault to find with the doctrine of retribution, as in his classic statement:

> Surely he repays humans according to their deeds,
> and brings upon them what their conduct deserves (34.11).

But the focus of his view of God lies elsewhere. For Elihu, God is the Great Communicator or Educator. When there is suffering, one is not to ask, What has this person done to deserve such punishment?, but What lesson is to be learned?, What has God to say through this affliction? Affliction is intended not for punishment but for deliverance:

> He delivers the afflicted by their affliction,
> and opens their ears by their distress (36.15).

Sometimes God uses dreams to warn people against committing sins they may be contemplating (33.15–18); at other times he sends sufferings for discipline, which lead, if rightly discerned, to deliverance for the sufferer (33.19–28). What is more, God's creatorial energies are not displays of power, but means of communication with his human creatures. When clouds and rain come, there is a message in them:

> Whether for correction, or for his land,
> or for loyalty, he dispatches them (37.13).

When the snows fall or the heavy rains, and humans are kept from their work, there is a message in that too:

> He shuts everyone indoors,
> so that all may recognize that he is at work (37.7).

And the thunder is his communication of his anger against wickedness:

> His thunder declares his wrath,
> the passion of his anger against iniquity (36.31).

God's educational intentions are for the improvement of humanity, and the inculcation of a proper attitude towards him as their deity. In sum, Elihu's theology is this:

> As for the Almighty, we cannot find him.
> Supreme in power, mighty in righteousness,
> he does not pervert justice.
> Therefore mortals fear him,
> and the wise in heart are afraid of him (37.23–24).

Which is to say, God is beyond human comprehension – though he is constantly conveying communications to humans – and utterly just, while supremely powerful. There is nothing cosy about his programme of education, however salvific it may be, for its purpose, we soon see, is to keep humans in their place. The only appropriate human response to what they come to learn about the divine is the emotion of fear (37.24); the fear of Yahweh, that is wisdom (28.28).

Elihu's theology decidedly goes beyond that of the other friends with their somewhat soulless retributionism, making a space for communication from the realm of the divine to the human. But his theology is still austere, and just as individualistically oriented, as theirs.

III. The voice of Job (Job 3; 6–7; 9–10; 12–14; 16–17; 19; 21; 22–24 [less 24.18–24]; 27.1–6, 11–12; 29–31; 40.3–4; 42.1–6)

Job, as a man who feared God and avoided evil (1.1), the very recipe for the good life urged by 28.28, had long accepted the theology of the three friends. His scrupulous, not to say over-anxious, piety that woke him each morning to offer sacrifice for his children in case they had offended God (1.5) is a narrative gesture to retributionist theology. But he has now experienced at first hand a refutation of that theology, in that he, who knows himself to be a just man, is being treated as a heinous sinner. His whole view of the justice of God is called into question, and he embarks on the most radical restatement of Israelite theology to be found in the pages of the Hebrew Bible.

Job's new theology is that God is a monster, motivated by cruelty and spite, who has not only attacked the innocent Job, but is also guilty of negligence and injustice on a universal scale. Job has no doubt that there is a god, for it is he who is wrongfully assaulting him; but he denies the goodness of that god.

Job's first instinct, trained as he has been in the piety of his day, has been to respond to the injustice of the assault on him from heaven with 'Yahweh gave, and Yahweh has taken away; blessed be the name of Yahweh' (1.21). This sadly fatalistic remark, which denatures any gift by making it revocable, is not long on Job's lips, for he is soon berating God for the disproportion of his wrath against him:

> Am I Sea, am I the monster Tannin,
>   that you keep me under guard? (7.12).
> What is humankind that you make so much of them,
>   fixing your mind upon them,

inspecting them every morning,
  at every moment testing them?
Will you never take your gaze from me,
  or let me be till I swallow my spittle? (7.17–19).

Foremost in Job's new theological vision is a developing concept of God as
gaoler, intrusive and suffocating, obsessed with destroying a human target
that can constitute no threat to his sovereignty:

If I have sinned how do I injure you,
  O Watcher of Humans?
Why have you set me up as your target?
  Why have I become a burden to you? (7.20).

Chief among the characteristics of this God is his anger. Being God, he does
not withdraw his anger (9.13a). The ancient myths were right, says Job,
when they recounted that the first thing God ever did was to create the world
by slaying the chaos monster in a primeval act of aggression (9.13b). And this
settled design of hostility towards his creation applies equally in the case
of the individual Job, who has been, since his conception, subject to the
cruelty of God:

Your hands fashioned me and made me;
  and now you have turned and destroyed me.
You moulded me like clay, do you remember?
  Now you turn me to mire again.
This was your secret intention,
  this was your purpose, I know,
that, if I sinned, you would be watching me
  and would not acquit me of my guilt! (10.8–9, 13–14).

What is God? If we are to talk theology, let us not overlook the testimony of
Job, a righteous man in the Hebrew tradition, to the reality of the divine:
God is a vicious enemy to an innocent mortal:

His anger has torn me, and his hatred assaults me;
  he gnashes his teeth at me.
  My enemy whets his eye at me.
I was untroubled, but he shattered me;
  he seized me by the neck and dashed me to pieces.

He made me his target;
  his bowmen surrounded me.
He pierced my kidneys; he was pitiless;
  he spilled my gall on the ground.
He battered me down, breach upon breach;
  he rushed against me like a champion (16.9, 12–14).

No urbane theological system should be allowed to obscure this witness to
the divine, and notably this witness from a man who is no enemy of religion
but is by all accounts God's boast and will be by God's own mouth acclaimed
as having spoken of him what is right (42.7)!

Job's charge against God goes further, however. In chs 23–24 especially,
his thought moves outwards from the injustice of his own sorry case to the
governance of the world itself. Here the essence of his argument is that God
does nothing to punish the wicked, and thus has abdicated moral responsibility for the world. The wicked can dispossess others of their livelihoods
with impunity; there is no retribution for them, and there is no justice for the
dispossessed any more than there is for Job:

Why are days of assize not kept by the Almighty?
  Why do those who know him not see his judgment days?
The wicked remove boundary-stones,
  they carry off flocks and pasture them as their own.
They drive away the donkey of the fatherless,
  and take the widow's bull as a pledge.
They force the needy off the road,
  and the poor of the land are utterly driven into hiding.
From the towns comes the groan of the dying,
  and the souls of the wounded cry out for help.
But God charges no one with wrong (24.1–4, 12).

That last line is the essence of Job's complaint. Not only are the righteous
and the deserving poor denied justice, but the wicked go scot free. There is
no retribution.

There is no denying that Job has been treated unjustly – so long as one
subscribes to the principle that the righteous deserve blessing. Job's
suffering is real enough, and it is cause enough for a cry to heaven. But his
suffering is not his greatest problem: it is the injustice of his suffering that
truly troubles him. Yet, truth to tell, Job is not so much God's victim as the
victim of his learned theology, which has led him to believe that he deserves

better. If there is no principle of retribution at work in the universe, he deserves nothing, and the only reward for his righteousness that he has a right to expect is the righteousness itself. Theology, however, has turned a terrible personal tragedy and physical distress into something far worse: disillusionment with God and the whole of the moral universe. It is time for another voice to speak, with a very different tone.

IV. The voice of Yahweh (Job 38–41)

Yahweh's speeches are famous for their refusal to address Job's questions. Their failure to respond to his problem is implicitly a refusal of the validity of his complaint. Yahweh does not say in so many words that Job is asking the wrong question or thinking in the wrong categories, but that is the implication of what he does say.

Whereas Job has put the issue of justice top of his agenda, Yahweh says nothing of justice, but speaks only of the structure and functioning of the universe. What he reproves Job for is setting his own agenda, without consideration of Yahweh's design for the world. His first words to Job are full of significance:

Who is this who obscures the Design
   by words without knowledge? (48.2).

Job's quest for justice, and his complaint that he is being denied it, obscure the fact that, according to these speeches, Yahweh does not undertake to ensure that justice reigns in the world. Yahweh has created the world, with its physical and moral systems, but he does not monitor the detail of what goes on it and he does not serve as a cosmic policeman. Job's insistence on justice to the neglect of other values has been darkening or obscuring the divine plan, preventing Yahweh's intentions from becoming apparent by his words that were creating an alternative world-view.

According to the discourse from the tempest, Job's questions, so central to his self-understanding and well-being, so influential also in the history of theological thought, are not interesting questions at all. There is a universal order, which Yahweh upholds ever since he instituted it at creation; but its principles are not balance and equity and retribution and equivalence, as Job and all the friends have thought. Its principles are more strategic than that. It majors on intimacy, on sustenance, on variety.

In this discourse, Yahweh knows his universe intimately. He knows how broad the earth is (38.18), the directions to the dwellings of light and darkness (38.19), the system of the stars (38.33), the birth cycle of mountain goats (39.1–3); he implants migratory instincts into birds (39.26) and maternal fecklessness into ostriches (39.16–17). This God is very wise – and he has a lot on his mind. He loves the detail, and, even when he is taking the broadest view, he only ever works with examples.

In this discourse, sustenance and nurture are key objectives of the universal order. Whether it is the physical universe or the animal world, the divine intimacy is directed to sustaining life. Creation is not just a past event for this world-view; every day the morning has to be remade by its creator, calling up the dawn, grasping the fringes of the earth, shaking the Dog-star from its place, bringing up the horizon in relief as clay under a seal till everything stands out like folds in a cloak and the light of the Dog-star is dimmed as the stars of the Navigator's line go out one by one (38.12–15). In this world-view, the god of all the earth is counting the months of each wild animal mother's pregnancy (39.2), imbuing wild horses with their strength (39.19), training hawks in flight (39.26), providing fresh meat for the young of eagles in their rocky fastnesses (39.27–30) and for young lions in their lairs (38.39–40), directing the raven to its quarry when its fledglings croak for lack of food (38.41).

In this discourse, the world is other and hugely various. It lives for itself, and if anything is instrumental, if anything serves a purpose other than itself, that is coincidental. The purposes of the universal structure are infinitely multiple, each of its elements with its own quiddity and its own mission – whether it is the sea, the clouds, light, darkness, rain, stars, mountain goat, ostrich, war-horse or eagle. Like Gerard Manley Hopkins's 'Pied Beauty', this vision evokes:

> Glory to God for dappled things
> For skies of couple-colour as a brinded cow
> Landscape plotted and pieced – fold, fallow, and plough;
> And all trades, their gear and tackle and trim.

This is a discourse without abstracts, without oppositions, without propositions, without generalizations. It works with images, and maximizes impact and affect. It has little time for clarity or logic. It is not the language of the *Summa* or the *Institutes*, or even of Deuteronomy or the dialogues of Job.

There is nothing about humans in the divine speeches, of course, nothing about ethics or justice or days of assize. That is talk for accountants; God's task is to be the leader and inspirer of the global enterprise. The divine speeches are his mission statement, his vision, the corporate thinking. The human is only one division of the global economy, and its specific problems cannot be given his top priority.

In the theology of the divine speeches, there is no problem with the world. Yahweh does not attempt a justification for anything that happens in the world of human affairs, and there is nothing that he needs to set right. The world is as he designed it. His world order does not ensure justice for the righteous or for evildoers, and he himself does not undertake to correct injustices in human affairs. Whereas Job regarded justice as a supreme value (perhaps the supreme value), the divine speeches may be said to put forward other competing values. In contemporary political philosophy, this would be called a situation of 'value pluralism' – such as in the conflicts between liberty and equality, or between loyalty to friends or to country. Value pluralism would suggest that even such a highly prized value as justice might be only one value among others, and that there may be no way to adjudicate all conflicts between values.

Finally, in the theology of the divine speeches lies an implicit answer to the Satan's question, Does Job serve God for naught? (1.9), with which the whole action of the narrative began. The question has indeed already been answered in the prologue, in the sense that Job continues to fear God even when the presumptive 'reward' of his piety, i.e. his prosperity, has been removed. He is proved to be pious 'without cause'. The Satan had suggested that he had a cause, that he was pious because he had found it paid to be pious: God had blessed him, and for that cause he reverenced God. Now in the divine speeches the question, Does Job serve God for naught?, is answered again, but in a different sense; for since they deny that there is a causal nexus between deed and consequence, it follows that every deed is done 'without cause', without any actual reward. No act, good or bad, has a payment or a reward attaching to it, for there is no principle of retribution at work in the universe. Since no one is rewarded for fearing God, Job too has not been rewarded for fearing God. It seems that the old theology of retribution has been finally laid to rest.

V. The narrator's voice (Job 1–2; 42.7–17)

Or has it? The last word in the Book of Job belongs not to Yahweh but to the narrator of the story, who is not at all unsophisticated theologically. And according to him, in ch. 1 Job feared God and avoided evil (1.1) and he was the greatest of all the easterners (1.4), as if we were reading of cause and effect, of the regular functioning of the principle of retribution. Now in ch. 42, hard on the heels of the divine abnegation of responsibility for retribution, the narrator assures us that Job, the one person who has spoken rightly of Yahweh (42.7–8), gets twice the wealth and the family he had at the beginning – his superlative piety, somewhat eccentrically expressed, to be sure, has led to his ultimate superlative prosperity. Can it be that what the book has been doing its best to demolish, the doctrine of retribution, is on its last page triumphantly affirmed?

We must admit that nothing in ch. 42 explicitly relates Job's final prosperity to his piety. We might even feel, having just now heard the divine speeches in which the principle of retribution has been entirely marginalized, if not explicitly denied, that the language of reward is conspicuous by its absence. Could it be simply that even the Yahweh of the speeches never denied himself the right to bless humans, and that his only resistance was to the assumption that he should and must if they fulfil certain conditions?

So why is Job restored? Within the logic, or the theology, of the book as it has by now developed, there is no reason. Yahweh does not need a reason, and Job has no right to expect anything of him. And yet – Job is a pious man, and Job is in the end, as he was in the beginning, a wealthy man, and fortunate as well in every other way. The doctrine of retribution has been negated, but does an afterglow still linger on?

VI. The author's voice (Job 1–42)

Six characters in search of a theology; so we might label the Book of Job. To the medley of their voices we should add another: the voice of the author. Which, among all the competing voices in the book, is most in tune with his own?

It may be that the author does not have a viewpoint that he wants to propound, that he is more of a poet than a theologian. What may interest him may be the play of opinion, the variety of plausible positions, the impossibility of definitive statement. The lyrical opportunities in his theme may be more important to him than reaching a satisfactory theological conclusion.

And yet it is tempting to imagine that he has a preference for one of the positions he has laid out so persuasively. At first, it seems impossible to believe that his sympathies do not lie with his hero Job; the passion and the drama of the book lie largely in the feelings and the words of this character. But, quite apart from the fact that the author has shown us that Job is labouring under a huge misapprehension about God throughout the whole of his speeches, can we believe that the 'viewpoint' of the book will turn out to be that of this injured man when another of the book's characters is none other than the deity? How could the viewpoint of the book be other than that of Yahweh himself?

And yet again there is something that makes one hesitate. It is the epilogue. It is not that the epilogue undermines the divine speeches, or affirms the principle of retribution by the back door, so to speak. It is the fact that the character Yahweh does not have the last word, but has to yield to the narrator. And what the narrator does in the closing chapter is to shift the focus from the grand designs of heaven to the petty domestic plane. The divine speeches have offered a heady vision of the universe and the principles that do or do not govern it. The final narrative narrows the focus astonishingly from the universal vision of chs 38–41 to a close-up of a doting father settling estates upon his daughters, of an amiable patriarch laying on banquets for all those visits of his extended family and acquaintances, of a master of animal husbandry adding to his enormous flocks year by year and putting them no doubt to profitable use. Has he given up his bombast in the town square (29.7–10)?, we wonder, and have his relations with the lower orders improved (30.1–2, 9–10)? With 22,000 animals and four generations of his own offspring to worry about, what time does he have left over for questions of cosmic theology?

What, in short, is important? That is a question that goes beyond any that have been raised already in the book. How to measure the relative value of a solution to the intellectual puzzle of the universe against the delight of dreaming up beautiful names for beautiful daughters? Every one of the characters in the book is the author's creation (including the character Yahweh, of course), but perhaps the narrator is closer to the author than any of them. Without negating for an instant the grand issues debated throughout the dialogues, could the author have had yet another vision of the human, one that did not hang upon questions of justice, but foregrounded the mundane, the domestic and the social business of living?

Note

The translations from Job are my own, and mostly the same as in my commentary, *Job*, Word Biblical Commentary 17; Waco, TX 1989; Word Biblical Commentary, 18A, 18B, Nashville 2004 (forthcoming). I have there explained my reasons for the attribution of various passages in the book to the different speakers.

II. Philosophical, Theological and Ethical Reflections

'We cannot fathom the Almighty.'
Defining the Relationship between Transcendence and Immanence in the Light of 'Job's God'

SASKIA WENDEL

The book of Job is generally regarded as an example of the way in which the Bible grapples with theodicy: why does the all-merciful and almighty, the good and righteous God of Israel, allow the innocent and the righteous to suffer? This grappling does not end with a solution to the theodicy question, but rather confirms that it is impossible to resolve; all questions and doubts fall dumb in the face of the omnipotence and unfathomability of the God who is highly exalted and beyond human control: 'The Almighty – we cannot fathom him; he is great in power and justice, and abundant righteousness he will not violate' (Job 37.23). What remains is simply to hope against all hope and to trust that the creator of the world and the God of the covenant will not abandon human beings – even through suffering and death. So at the end of the book of Job there is the 'leap of faith' and the acknowledgment of the divine mystery which ultimate escapes all human capacity for knowledge: 'I know that you can do all things, and that no purpose of yours can be thwarted. Who is this that hides counsel without knowledge? Therefore I have uttered what I did not understand, things too wonderful for me, which I did not know' (Job 42.3).

However, this answer to the theodicy question indicates another problem. This problem is not stated explicitly in the book of Job, but becomes its implicit theme: it is the problem of the relationship between God and the world, or in philosophical terms the problem of defining the relationship between infinite and finite, transcendence and immanence. For the answer given in the book of Job presupposes a definition of this relationship which is dominated by the difference between God and the world and by the way in which God is withdrawn and outside human control: an epistemological definition of the relationship is inferred from the metaphysical definition, and the thesis about theodicy is in turn based on this.

Here I want to use the definition of the relationship between transcendence and immanence given in the book of Job as the occasion for discussing the relationship between transcendence and immanence from a philosophical perspective. To do this, however, it is necessary first to give a closer definition of the term 'transcendence' which stands at the centre of the following remarks.

I. The concept of transcendence and the idea of the unconditional

As is well known, the terms 'transcendence' or 'transcend' are derived from the Latin verb *transcendere*, which initially means simply a passing over, a going-beyond-something or an ascent to what is 'more' and 'over and above'.[1] Both 'transcending' as the activity of surpassing and 'transcendence' as the 'over and above' and thus the whither of the transcending can be interpreted in different ways. First the 'more' can be understood as a 'more' or 'beyond' which is so to speak within the world, a 'more' as a part and moment of being-in-the-world: for example, another person can be understood as a 'more' in approaching whom the self surpasses itself, and so can a historical circumstance which goes beyond the social status quo. Theodor Wiesengrund Adorno and Ernst Bloch speak of transcendence in the latter sense: for Adorno, the term 'transcendence' denotes a 'more' which is something that goes beyond the purely factual but which belongs to the immanence and contingency of being-in-the-world; this is expressed in a work of art.[2] According to Adorno, this 'more' cannot formulate a utopia, since it is not in any way the idea of a 'wholly otherness' of facticity, but the idea of how it could be but is not. Likewise Ernst Bloch speaks of the possibility of a 'transcending without transcendence';[3] here unlike Adorno he maintains the idea of a 'more' in the sense of a utopian state of consummation, but sees this as a part and moment of the world or history.[4]

Contrasting with this understanding of 'transcending' as the activity of self-surpassing and 'transcendence' in the sense of a 'more' within the world is an understanding of transcending and transcendence which understands transcending as a surpassing towards an 'over and above' which is no longer exclusively a part and moment of being-in-the-world, in other words which is no longer to be understood as transcendence merely within the world. Here, rather, 'transcendence' is defined in the sense of an infinite and/or unconditioned which goes beyond the finitude and conditioned nature of the world and surpasses it. The movement of transcending already participates in this surpassing of the world in principle. This understanding of transcendence can be both about the idea of an unconditioned which need not necessarily correspond with the idea of the existence of this unconditioned, and also about the idea of another reality which surpasses the conditioned state of being-in-the-world.[5] The latter notion is decisive for our context, namely the reference to a 'more' which not only transcends one's own Dasein in the direction of another Dasein or other historical situations but surpasses being-in-the-world as a whole. This transcending towards a whither which is at the same time is defined as the whence of the world and human beings, which surpasses the finitude and conditioned state of the world, characterizes the religious understanding of transcendence, which is distinct from other notions of transcendence in the sense of surpassings within the world and which accordingly also underlies the biblical understanding of transcendence. However, if we start from this understanding of transcendence, we have to ask how precisely we are to define the whence which at the same time is whither, and then go on from there to investigate the definition of the relationship between transcendence and immanence.

It seems natural to identify the concept of transcendence with that of the infinite: that whither the I surpasses itself in its being-in-the-world is the infinite which is the ground, original and goal, the whence and whither of the infinite, contingent being-in-the-world. The infinite is already inscribed on our reason as the idea of the infinite; Descartes, for example, drew attention to this in the third of his *Meditations on the First Philosophy*.[6] But when examined closely, the concept of the infinite proves to be too unspecific for it to be capable of defining the concept of transcendence used in the religious context. For infinity *per se* does not make the 'over and above' a more which surpasses being-in-the-world as a whole, nor is it convincing to identify infinity with an 'over and above' in the sense of a 'more'. For example, matter, too, can be understood as infinite, or the 'infinite expanses' of the universe. Similarly, nothingness cannot be identified with the infinite whither human Dasein transcends itself. However, nothingness as the whither of that transcending would not be a 'more', something 'over and above' this existence; on the contrary it would be its extinction, its annihilation.[7] In the face of these naturalistic or nihilistic possibilities of interpreting the concept of the infinite, we shall have to identify the concept of transcendence in religious terms more with the concept of the unconditioned than with that of the infinite; otherwise the definition of the concept would be imprecise and self-contradictory. The concept of the unconditioned, not that of the infinite, corresponds with the idea of perfection intended by Descartes, which is always already inscribed on the reason, and on the basis of which the conditioned, the contingent, can first of all be identified and named as such. Religious convictions feed on this idea of the unconditioned, but in those very convictions it is not only postulated as an idea but is also believed to exist. This conviction implies the ontological obligation to postulate the unconditioned not only as an epistemologically and/or ethically necessary idea, for example in terms of transcendental logic as an unconditioned I, as unconditioned knowledge, as unconditioned freedom or as an unconditioned ought, but also to attribute the unconditioned to existence – as unconditioned being. This unconditioned as the whence and whither of contingent existence can be understood theistically, as in Judaism, Christianity and Islam, as one single personal God – here unconditioned being is related to an unconditioned I and to unconditioned freedom. But it can also be interpreted non-theistically; in that case the alternative is a monistic interpretation of the unconditioned or the 'over and above' at the centre of which stands the notion of all-unity, which is open both to polytheistic interpretations and also to pantheistic or panentheistic interpretations.[8]

If we now define transcendence as a 'more' or an 'over and above' in the sense of an unconditioned, the question arises how to define the relationship between transcendence and immanence, the unconditioned and the conditioned – a definition which is also decisive for the book of Job and its understanding of God.

II. 'Job's God': absolute transcendence of the unconditioned?

In the book of Job we first encounter a definition of the relationship between transcendence and immanence based on a particular understanding of transcendence: transcendence is identified with the unconditioned, but over against the conditioned this is an other. As such, transcendence is radically different from immanence, and being unconditioned is absolutely different from being conditioned. This strict separation of transcendence and immanence, unconditioned and conditioned, implies several characteristics of transcendence: it is radically and absolutely withdrawn from the conditioned, so at the same time it is radical absence. Accordingly it is absolute mystery and as such is ineffable, unknowable. However, since transcendence and immanence are radically different, transcendence, the unconditioned, is 'beyond' the conditioned entity; 'beyond' human thought, feeling and will; 'beyond' the immanence of being-in-the-world. It can even be understood as a 'beyond Being' in so far as Being always still remains imprisoned in being conditioned, immanence. This understanding of transcendence can refer to a corresponding understanding of transcendence in the philosophical tradition, which becomes differentiated in two directions. A first direction identifies transcendence in the Neoplatonic tradition with the One, from which Being and its hypostases spirit, soul and matter all first all originate.[9] In the tradition of negative theology which originates in both Judaism and Christianity the One that cannot be named or known and is hidden in 'mystical darkness' is identified with the ineffable God – as distinct from the God who reveals himself, whose divine ground is the Godhead. A second direction, represented above all in parts of French phenomenology and in postmodern or post-structuralist concepts, radicalizes this tradition and identifies transcendence not with the One but – as the radically Other over against the immanent in its being unconditioned – with alterity. Here it is neither a reified entity which can be hypostatized to a supreme being, nor Being. In distinction from Heidegger's thesis of the ontological difference between Being and entity, here the Other is understood rather as the Other of Being, and as such as transcendence. Emmanuel Lévinas puts it like this: 'If transcendence has a meaning, then for the event of Being – for the *esse* – for *being* (*essence*) – this can only mean going over to the Other of Being.'[10] This radical transcendence of the absolutely Other is a past which cannot be thought of beforehand and an absence which cannot be made present: it escapes any possibility of being made present (again).[11] So it is an abiding mystery: ineffable, inconceivable, unimaginable.[12] For Lévinas, radical alterity is identical with the Cartesian idea of the infinite: 'The otherness of the Other is not annulled, it does not get fused into the thought that it thinks. In thinking the infinite, the I *a priori* thinks more than it thinks. The infinite is not completely comprehended in the idea of the infinite, is not understood; this idea is not a concept. The infinite is the radically, the absolutely Other. The transcendence of the infinite over against me, whom am separated from it and think it, represents the first sign of its infinity.'[13] Like Lévinas, Jacques Derrida and Jean-François Lyotard also define alterity as a radical and absolute otherness, but they do not identify it with the idea of the infinite. Derrida relates it to the ineffable event, or to the gift and the *différance*[14] in reference and to the *chora*: 'It is not Being, not goodness, not God, not the human being, not history. It will constantly oppose these authorities, it will constantly have been the place of an infinite resistance, an infinitely insensitive and unshakable remainder: a wholly other that has no face...'[15] Lyotard identifies that alterity with an indescribable absolute obligation which is event and gift at the same time.[16]

At most this radical alterity can be presented in a negative way as a trace, as a sign – not as a sign of something designated but as the expression of a perpetual withdrawal: for Lévinas, for example, transcendence breaks into immanence as a 'trace of the infinite, which *passes by* without being able to enter – the trace of an absence'.[17] It does so in the countenance of the other as an expression, as an epiphany of the other. Yet here transcendence is never taken up into immanence without remainder, nor does it come to appearance in it: 'The God who has passed by is not the original of which the countenance would be the copy.'[18] Likewise, for Derrida the radical absence can be presented only as a trace, and Lyotard too emphasizes the impossibility of depicting the law or the event, which at most can be presented in the mode of a negative depiction, in other words the depiction of the impossibility of its being depicted.[19] According to Lyotard, there are several such traces or negative depictions of that which can never be depicted. One of these traces is the 'soundless' letter of the *torah*, scripture, *miqra*;[20] another is the tetragrammaton, inexpressible name, which is not the name of a divine being but in its inexpressibility is an expression of the inexpressible itself.[21]

Now there is a variant of this understanding of transcendence in the book of Job: God is identified with an alterity which is separate from the immanence of the world. God is the creator of the world, and accordingly there is an irresolvable difference between creator and creature, between transcendence and immanence. The unfathomable nature of the creator is grounded in the difference in creation; in his loftiness and his greatness God escapes the conditioned knowledge of the creature. But by comparison with the philosophical concept of radical alterity 'Job's God' is also distinct from the idea of radical alterity. God is the unconditioned, the unconditioned I and unconditioned freedom (as the creator, sustainer and perfecter of the world), and also unconditioned Being (as the ground of the created entity), and as such at the same time person, since he stands in relation to the conditioned which has been created by it. Thus God is no absolute transcendence in the sense of radical alterity and absence, since God shows himself in history, reveals himself in his creation and shares himself with human beings. The unconditioned, though different from the conditioned, shows itself in the conditioned, is present in it without being taken up into it without remainder. So in Job we can note a peculiar tension in the definition of the relationship between the transcendence and the immanence of God: on the one hand an emphasis on the absolute transcendence of God and the 'leap of faith' that results from it, in order to be able to repel the problem of theodicy, and on the other an emphasis on the creative action of God, in particular in order to be able to emphasize the loftiness and greatness of the creator over against the creature. Moreover philosophical and theological interpretations of Job could succumb to the temptation to resolve this tension by embedding 'Job's God' in the concept of radical alterity, so as to clarify the concept of transcendence and to use that definition of transcendence as an explicit basic legitimation for settling the problem of theodicy. Job also intends this. However, it seems problematical both philosophically and theologically.

Philosophically the aspect of the radical separation of the unconditioned and the conditioned needs to be criticized: the unconditioned is devoid of any materiality, any historicity, and can never, indeed may never, appear in history, may never posses a material content. It cannot communicate itself in and through the conditioned, since the unconditioned and conditioned are not connected. But this perspective implies a residuary dualism, because the unconditioned can never materialize, never assume a body, never become history. Moreover without any possibility of mediation, the basic connection between the unconditioned and conditioned is lost, though it is this to which the idea of the unconditioned in the conditioned points: the conditioned is recognized as being conditioned on the basis of the idea of the unconditioned. Dasein recognizes itself as being conditioned through its knowledge of the unconditioned, and at the same time recognizes in the unconditioned its own ground to which it owes itself. If there were no mediation between the two, the conditioned would not know that it was conditioned, nor would it know the ground, the whither and whence, of its being conditioned, and thus ultimately would know nothing at all about the unconditioned. Without the reciprocal mediation of transcendence and immanence, the unconditioned and the conditioned, there would be no epiphany of the other at all. The other, transcendence, the unconditioned, would ultimately sublate itself were it not related to that and mediated with that whose 'more', whose other, it is. What, moreover, would distinguish the radical alterity as being beyond Being from the radical nothingness of Nietzschean provenance? What would distinguish it from the idea of a radical 'outside' which, as say Jacques Lacan and Michel Foucault had pointed out, could not be other than the result of mechanisms of repression within discursive practices? In that case, would not radical alterity again prove to be a 'more' within the world which in the unquenchable act of desire for a 'great' transcendence is hypostatized into such a transcendence as an act of 'transcending without transcendence'? In addition, the assertion of the radical transcendence and absence of the unconditioned implies an equivocal perspective with respect to the possibility of knowing the unconditioned and speaking of it, and from that ultimately follows the random nature of the definition of the concept of the unconditioned or of transcendence, since if there were no certainty that these two concepts corresponded, the concept of the unconditioned could, say, be detached from that of perfection.

These philosophical problems in the concept of alterity become further accentuated theologically, for the belief in one God which is confessed in the Jewish-Christian tradition with reference to the biblical testimony becomes fragile in a concept of radical alterity: faith in one God who has created the world in freedom and relates to it in his communication of himself. Moreover that very understanding of God becomes arbitrary if knowledge of God and talk of God are equivocal. Contrary to the biblical testimony, God could also be a malign genius, a deceiver who was almighty but cunning, who delights in deceiving human beings, an arbitrary God who where possible idolizes himself by means of human suffering and keeps imposing new suffering on human beings.[22] It is striking that in the book of Job, too, regardless of the conviction of the unfathomability of God an understanding of God is advocated which gives God predicates like righteousness, loftiness or omnipotence. If we nevertheless wanted to maintain this understanding of God in the face of the equivocal nature of talk of God, ultimately it could not be justified by reason, but only asserted fideistically through a 'leap of faith'. Moreover that leap of faith and thus the leap into a radically negative theology appears at the end of the book of Job as the only possible of avoiding the question of theodicy. This leap may seem plausible if one conjectures a horribly deep ditch between reason and faith which can be crossed only by such a leap, and if one is convinced that because of human finitude and guilt human beings are themselves already disfigured by radical evil, indeed that reason itself is already the root of hybris against God, sin. But if one is convinced that reason is a gift and image of God in which God communicates himself – an image which is marked by being conditioned and imperfect, but which can never be completely obscured since it is God's gift, one will not see any opposition between reason and faith, but a mediating relationship.[23] In that case a 'leap of faith' is ruled out: rather, a responsive and responsible faith must be able to justify its conviction by way of reason, otherwise it would be sheer ideology. If it were against reason to believe in a just God, the question would remain why human beings should hang on to such an unreasonable faith at all, in particular in the face of the problem of theodicy.[24]

So given the inconsistency of the concept of radical alterity, it does not seem plausible to resolve the tension in Job's understanding of transcendence by identifying 'Job's God' exclusively with radical alterity. Instead, I want to sketch out a philosophical definition of the relationship between transcendence and immanence which can do more justice than the concept of radical alterity to the tension between transcendence and immanence, the presence and absence of the unconditioned in the conditioned, which is also expressed in the book of Job regardless of the conviction of the otherness of God.

III. Transcendence and immanence as a mediating relationship: the unconditioned as a moment of the conditioned

If we understand 'transcendence' in religious terms in the sense of a 'more' or 'over and above' which surpasses contingent being-in-the-world as a whole as its whence and whither, then, as I have already explained, we will have to identify the concept of 'transcendence' with that of the unconditioned on the basis of which the conditioned can first be defined as conditioned. The definition of the relationship between transcendence and immanence is thus connected with the definition of the relationship between unconditioned and conditioned. That definition of the relationship between unconditioned and conditioned in turn points to a further relationship, namely to the relationship between the universal and the individual or particular. For there is a relationship between the concept of the unconditioned and that of a universal, just as there is a relationship between the concept of the conditioned and that of the individual and peculiar: as individual and particular the individual is at the same time conditioned and contingent. The individual is limited by another individual, and like another individual is finite. The universal cannot therefore be as conditioned as the individual; rather, it is unconditioned, since in the end it is limited neither as an individual nor through an individual. The definition of the relationship between the universal and the individual therefore makes it possible to make an inference to the relationship between the unconditioned and the conditioned and thus also to that between transcendence and immanence. But if, first, we want to think about the unconditioned and the conditioned not as a relationship of radical difference or alterity but as a mediating relationship and, secondly, want to define this relationship in connection with the insights of the linguistic turn neither as a relationship of representation nor as a mere relationship of participation of Platonic origin, it is necessary to relate the unconditioned and the conditioned, transcendence and immanence, to each other in such a way that the unconditioned is not thought of alongside or above the conditioned, but in it.[25] In an ontological perspective this thesis has already been put forward in the context of the discussion of the ontological status of the universal: the universal is something in or of individual things, namely their basis and origin which never exists in detachment from the individual thing but is not itself a singular thing, for things cannot be predicated of another thing; only properties can be predicated of a thing. The universal is not a thing at all in the sense of a substance or nature, but a moment of and in the individual thing.[26] Now this definition of the universal as a moment of the individual and special can also be transferred to the definition of the relationship between the unconditioned and the conditioned or transcendence and immanence. The unconditioned would then need to be understood as an element in and of the conditioned, not just ontologically with relation to the concept of being, but also in terms of transcendental logic as, say, a moment of an unconditioned feeling of obligation which arises in the conditioned state of a concrete situation for action, within a decision in an individual case. Defined in such a way, the unconditioned has a reference to history, to being conditioned, to the immanence of human existence: in the midst of history and contingency, in the midst of the incompleteness of what is, something appears which is more than what is: 'There is no light on human beings and things in which transcendence is not reflected. Inexorably opposed to the fungible world of the exchange is that of the eye which does not want the colours of the world to be destroyed. The unseeming promises itself in the seeming.'[27] The concept of 'transcendence', then, does not denote any radical alterity of immanence, any absolute absence, any beyond Being, but the moment of being unconditioned that comes to appearance in the conditioned state of finite existence. This unconditioned is not an entity, and is therefore an other over against the entity; however, likewise it is not beyond Being and therefore is not a radically, absolutely other over against being-in-the-world and the entity. On the contrary, in its coming-to-appearance it also shows itself as that which is not the other and thus as other and not-other at the same time – a tension which likewise is expressed in the concept of the moment. In this way transcendence is expressed not only as a trace but as an appearance, as an apparition of transcendence in immanence. But this apparition does not come about as a direct, unmediated presentation of transcendence; it is not directly present, for transcendence comes to appearance only as a moment, and this character of moment implies a simultaneity of presence and absence, corresponding to the simultaneity of otherness and not-otherness. In the moment of the coming-to-appearance of transcendence it hides itself, for it never appears directly and immediately, but always already broken and communicated in brokenness, the finitude and conditioned state of history. 'No notion of transcendence is more possible than by dint of transitoriness; eternity does not appear as such but broken through that which is most transitory.'[28] There is a difference between the unconditioned and the conditioned; nevertheless there is mediation between the two in the moment of the appearance of the unconditioned in the conditioned – a moment that unites what is distinguished as a constellation, but without sublating it in terms of the logic of identity into an all-embracing unity and thus dissolving the difference between unconditioned and conditioned. The showing of itself by the unconditioned is thus at the same time and always already a withdrawing – and precisely in that it is also a 'more' and 'over and above' the facticity of the entity, yet it is more than the mere trace of an absence which can never show itself.[29]

That definition of transcendence as a moment of immanence has consequences for the definition of the possibility of knowledge of and talk about transcendence. That talk cannot be either univocal or equivocal, because on the one hand transcendence is not an entity and therefore never presents itself directly in the mode of an entity and so can never be defined univocally,[30] and on the other hand in its coming-to-appearance it never completely evades and closes itself to the human capacity for knowledge.[31] Accordingly, we have to understand talk about transcendence in analogy to the mediating relationship between transcendence and immanence.[32] As is well known, talking of God by way of analogy in no way scorns the mystery and the holiness of God, but it does stress the possibility in the face of the holiness of God of nevertheless being able to speak of God – by way of analogy, as the formula of the Fourth Lateran Council put it in a way which is better than anything yet: '… one cannot establish such a great similarity between the creator and the creature that no even greater dissimilarity between them could be established'.[33]

Now if we relate that definition of transcendence and immanence once again to Job, despite the emphasis on the otherness of God in the book of Job a correspondence can also be established between 'Job's God' and the definition of transcendence and immanence sketched out here because on the one hand 'Job's God' as an abiding mystery can never put himself in the picture directly and without mediation, but on the other hand – though he is not an entity – he is not beyond Being and history but shows himself in creation, in history. God relates himself to his creatures, shares himself with them and promises himself without making himself available. In this perspective the tension noted in 'Job's God' thus proves not to be a contradiction to be overcome but even an expression of the mediating relationship between transcendence and immanence, the unconditioned and the conditioned. However, there would be too much harmony were one to tone down the break between on the one hand the plea for a mediating relationship between transcendence and immanence and the plea for the possibility which follows from this and on the other the rejection of the problem of theodicy at the end of the book of Job. Under the pressure of theodicy the book of Job then succumbs to the temptation of surrendering the tense mediating relationship between transcendence and immanence in favour of emphasis on the unfathomability of God. But perhaps precisely in view of the radical character of the theodicy question it is necessary not to break off the way of thought dogmatically by a leap of faith which is both philosophically and theologically questionable, but precisely in view of 'Job's God' once again to venture a theodicy, not least in view of the dangers which are undoubtedly incurred with such a project. Here an epistemologically orientated discussion of the relationship between transcendence and immanence which is not exclusively orientated on the concept of radical otherness could be of decisive importance.

Translated by John Bowden

Notes

1. Cf. Jens Halfwassen, 'Transzendenz; Transzendieren', in *Historisches Wörterbuch der Philosophie* 10, ed. Joachim Ritter and Karlfried Gründer, Basle 1998, pp. 1442ff.
2. Cf. e.g. Theodor W. Adorno, *Ästhetische Theorie*, Frankfurt am Main ¹³1993, p. 200.
3. Ernst Bloch, *Das Prinzip Hoffnung*, Frankfurt am Main 1973, p. 1522.
4. Martin Heidegger's understanding of transcendence can also be interpreted in this way. Dasein transcends itself ecstatically in listening to the speaking of Being which addresses it. So in the hearing and accepting of the claim of Being there is a movement of transcending; however, looked at precisely, the whither of this transcending, transcendence, is not an other of Being or the being-in-the-world of Dasein, but the world in which Dasein lives and towards which it ek-sists, as well as Being itself, which shows itself in the entity that encounters Dasein as being-in-the-world and that discloses itself in the perception of being. For this see e.g. Martin Heidegger, *Sein und Zeit*, Tübingen ¹⁶1986, pp. 350–66.
5. For this differentiation of the concept of transcendence see also the sociological definition of the concept in Thomas Luckmann, who distinguishes between 'small', 'medium' and 'great' transcendences. Whereas 'small' and 'medium' transcendences are always related to everyday experiences, we need to speak of 'great' transcendences when it is a question of relationship to another reality which breaks out of and transcends the realm of everyday experience. Cf. e.g.

Thomas Luckmann, 'Privatisierung und Individualisierung. Zur Sozialform der Religion in spätindustriellen Gesellschaften', in Karl Gabriel (ed.*)*, *Religiöse Individualisierung und Säkularisierung. Biographie und Gruppe als Bezugspunkte moderner Religiosität*, Gütersloh 1996, pp. 17–28: 20.

6. Cf. René Descartes, *Meditationes de prima philosophia*, III, 28ff.

7. For the infinity of nothingness cf. e.g. Friedrich Nietzsche, *Ecce homo. Kritische-Studien-Ausgabe 6*, ed. Giorgio Colli und Mazzino Montinari, Munich 1999, p. 297.

8. However, in monistic interpretations there is again a tendency to identify the unconditioned with the infinite: with the infinity of the divine All-One, with the infinity of the universe as the mode of this All-Oneness, with the eternal return of the coming into being and passing away of the world in and through the divine All-Oneness. There is a problematical analogy here between monistic interpretations of the unconditional in the sense of the infinite and naturalistic or nihilistic interpretations of the infinite.

9. Cf. e.g. Plotinus, *Enneads* V 4, 2f.

10. Emmanuel Lévinas, *Autrement qu' être ou au-dela de l'essence*, La Haye 1974, p. 3.

11. Cf. ibid., pp. 11, 14.

12. Cf. e.g. Emmanuel Lévinas, *Totalité et infini. Essai sur l'extériorité*, La Haye 1971, pp. 50f.

13. Emmanuel Lévinas, *Die Spur des Anderen. Untersuchungen zur Phänomenologie und Sozialphilosophie*, Munich and Freiburg 1983, p. 197.

14. On this cf. e.g. Jacques Derrida, *Donner le temps. 1. La fausse monnaie*, Paris 1991, pp. 27ff. and 47ff.

15. Jacques Derrida, 'Glaube und Wissen. Die beiden Quellen der "Religion" an den Grenzen der bloßen Vernunft', in id. and Gianni Vattimo, *Die Religion*, Frankfurt am Main 2001, p. 37.

16. Cf. e.g. Jean-François Lyotard and Jean-Luc Thébaud, *Au Juste. Conversations*, Paris 1979, p. 102.

17. Lévinas, *Autrement qu'être* (n.20), p. 118.

18. Lévinas, *Die Spur des Anderen* (n.13), p. 235.

19. Cf. here e.g. Jean-François Lyotard, 'Vorstellung, Darstellung, Undarstellbarkeit', in id., *Immaterialität und Postmoderne*, Berlin 1985, pp. 91–102: 98.

20. Jean-François Lyotard, 'Von einem Bindestrich (D'un trait d'union)', in id. and Eberhard Gruber, *Ein Bindestrich. Zwischen "Jüdischem" und "Christlichem"*, enlarged edition Düsseldorf and Bonn 1995, pp. 27–51: 27.

21. Cf. Lyotard and Gruber (n.20), pp. 102f.

22. For this critique of a radical negative theology and an equivocal understanding of theology precisely in the context of the question of theodicy cf. e.g. Armin Kreiner, *Gott im Leid. Zur Stichhaltigkeit der Theodizee-Argumente*, Freiburg, Basle and Vienna 1997, pp. 56–78; Karl-Heinz Menke, 'Der Gott, der jetzt

schon Zukunft schenkt. Plädoyer für eine christologische Theodizee', in Harald Wagner (ed.), *Mit Gott streiten. Neue Zugänge zum Theodizee-Problem*, Freiburg, Basle and Vienna 1998, pp. 90–130, esp. 96ff.; Magnus Striet, *Offenbares Geheimnis. Zur Kritik der negativen Theologie*, Regensburg 2003, pp. 27–31.

23. Cf. here, with a reference to Anselm of Canterbury's programme of a *ratio fidei*, e.g. Hansjürgen Verweyen, *Gottes letztes Wort. Grundriss der Fundamentaltheologie*, Regensburg ³2000, pp. 37–57.

24. Cf. here also Striet, *Offenbares Geheimnis* (n.22), 30: ' . . . at least it must be possible to predicate morality of God as a minimal definition, in order to provide moral legitimation for faith in him in view of the harsh questions which arise from the arsenal of the theodicy question. And neither faith nor theology can be dispensed from this duty of legitimation, if it is also to be the case that an account of the hope which supports faith is to be given to *all* who ask, and the *fides qua creditur* is not to be lightly separated from the *fides quae creditur*, a separation which it cannot endure for long.'

25. Thus the definition of the relationship between transcendence and immanence which is sketched out below is orientated on two presuppositions: on the one hand a critique of the concept of radical otherness and on the other a critique of a metaphysics of presence and a monistic notion of the all-unity which is bound up with this metaphysic, as the notion of all-oneness includes the notion of the omnipresence of the All-One. Among other things, the metaphysics of presence is problematical because of its thesis of the possibility of the direct presentation of the Absolute, which implies the possibility of direct knowledge and that what presents itself directly is at our disposal. The notion of all-unity is in turn to be criticized because in it not only is the difference between the unconditioned and the conditioned, the universal and the individual, the particular, levelled down, but it follows a basic pattern in the logic of identity in which the indvidual is robbed of its independence and ultimately taken up into an all-embracing all-unity. As a result of this, looked at closely, the individual loses its uniqueness and is reduced to the mere status of a mode of the universal. This criticism of monism and the metaphysic of presence bound up with it cannot be investigated further here.

26. The mediation between the universal and the particular takes place in and as moment – a notion which also appears in Hegel; however, for him this is not the universal movement of the particular but on the contrary the particular moment of the universal, into which it is ultimately sublated. Thus in Hegel the difference between universal and particular is done away with and along with it the independent existence of the individual over against the universal. Here, by contrast, the independent state of the individual is preserved, as is the difference between universal and individual, since while the universal appears as a moment of the individual, as a phenomenon it is not dissolved in the individual.

27. Theodor W. Adorno, *Negative Dialektik*, Frankfurt am Main ⁵1988, pp. 396f.

28. Ibid., p. 353. The question of the mode of this appearance can be answered by means of a concept of the image which differes from Plato's idea of the image: the unconditional apppears as an image which is not a mere copy of an original, but in which the unconditioned is completely and fully contained. Nevertheless the unconditioned does not present itself directly in the image but – as an image – in the mode of a mediated immediacy in the tension of a presence which at the same time withdraws itself and in so doing is absent. For this concept of the image in connection with Meister Eckhart and Fichte see the detailed discussion by Saskia Wendel, *Affektiv und inkarniert. Ansätze Deutscher Mystik als subjekttheoretische Herausforderung*, Regensburg 2002, esp. pp. 195–209. For the parallels between this concept of the image and the understanding of symbols in the Kabbala in distinction from postmodern theories of the absence of the absolute, cf. e.g. ead., 'Jean-François Lyotard – Zeugnis für das Undarstellbare', in Joachim Valentin and Saskia Wendel (eds), *Jüdische Traditionen in der Philosophie des 20. Jahrhunderts*, Darmstadt 2000, pp. 264–78: 269ff.

29. For this tension between presence and absence, nearness and distance in the moment of showing the self cf. e.g. Martin Heidegger, 'Der Spruch des Anaximander', in id., *Holzwege*, Frankfurt am Main ⁷1994, pp. 321–73: 347; id., 'Zeit und Sein', in id., *Zur Sache des Denkens*, Tübingen 1988, pp. 1–25: 16. Cf. also Adorno, *Negative Dialektik* (n.27), 385.

30. So there is a difference between what shows itself and what 'is the case'. What shows itself escapes the grasp of conceptual thinking, discursive knowledge, by contrast with what is the case. Therefore it cannot be expressed univocally either. Nevertheless what shows itself also wants to be said: it presses into the realm of the discursive but can never be completely comprehended by it. The mode of this talk about what shows itself is analogy.

31. This becomes especially plausible if one can make out a moment of the unconditioned in the conditioned state of human existence itself in which the unconditioned comes into the picture, say in the subjectivity and freedom of the concrete individual. For this see e.g. Wendel, *Affektiv und inkarniert* (n.28).

32. For analogy as the middle way between equivocal and univocal cf. e.g. Thomas Aquinas, *Summa theologica* I, 13, 5c.

33. DH 806. However, it has to be emphasized that under the condition of the linguistic turn the possibility of the analogy can no longer be justified ontologically with reference to the assumption of an *analogia entis*, but has to be justified in terms of linguistic theology with reference to Wittgenstein's thesis that the meaning of language arises through usage. What is in principle an infinite chain of meanings finds both the condition of its possibility and its limitation in a principle on which it is grounded, but which is not itself a member of this chain.

Who is Responsible?

HERMANN HÄRING

I. Experiences of the insoluble

On a visit to the United States, as usual I was thoroughly cross-examined at the airport. The official, an elderly gentleman of colour, discovered that I was on my way to a theological seminar. He told me firmly that before entering the country I had to answer an important question for him: 'What is the most beautiful book in the Bible?' I hesitated. 'Song of Solomon' was on the tip of my tongue. But then I changed my mind and said, 'the book of Job'. Fortunately, he smiled with pleasure at my reply, showed me a photo of his pastor and told me that God was on our side especially in times of misfortune, but that along with Job we might complain and weep. There was no point in asking who was responsible and apportioning blame. He said that he had always trusted in God and God had always helped him, even when things were not going well.

That was not the time to enter into a theological dispute with so sympathetic a fellow Christian. At any rate I felt ashamed of myself because the question of God's responsibility nevertheless continued to perplex me. I could not have given such a convincing answer from the bottom of my heart. But does that mean that I must have a bad conscience? I've often tried to answer this question with the Bible in my hand.[1] In it I have read that Yahweh himself hardened the heart of the Pharaohs (Ex.10.1) and the heart of the people (Isa.6.10). I have noted that Yahweh can again shatter his people, just as the potter shatters the bowl which he has made (Isa.45.9; Jer.18.6). The book of Isaiah has taught me that Yahweh forms the light and creates darkness, that he brings about salvation and causes disaster (Isa.45.7). Moreover if systematic theology is right in claiming that according to scripture God has created everything, then we cannot remove evil from God's ultimate responsibility either. But how can the good God call evil to life? I know that Augustine found a brilliant solution to this dilemma: evil is really nothing, what is at work is only a 'lack of good'(Latin *privatio boni*). But at the same time Augustine has told us that evil is not to be sought at the level of an entity but at the levels of activity and effect. So regardless of whether evil does or does not exist, there is destruction and death: 'That is bad and wicked which harms us'.[2] Thus the definition of evil as a lack (which completely exonerates God) is as it were a boundary statement, like what is said in Isa.6.9f., and puts all the blame on Yahweh:

> Go and say to this people:
> 'Hear and hear, but do not understand;
> see and see, but do not perceive.'
> Make the heart of this people fat,
> And their ears heavy,
> And shut their eyes;
> Lest they see with their eyes,
> And hear with their ears,
> And understand with their hearts,
> And turn and be healed.

So we have two opposing, contradictory statements. The first explains evil with decisive certainty and philosophical skill as nothing, although the power of evil is manifest. The second declares that Yahweh is the cause of evil, although it is Yahweh himself who makes people impotent. Karl Barth declares evil (contrary to all the rules of logic) to be 'nothingness', a third between being and nothingness, because he want to take evil seriously and at the same time save God's power.[3] These are evidently limit statements and limit experiences particularly for those who want to understand their existence in terms of the goodness of God. In such statements both belief in God's good creation and the call to take evil with radical seriousness miss the mark and break apart the rules of our consistent everyday thought.

Can we then solve the problem by understanding evil as punishment for a wicked action? Certainly, in that case God's purposes and human purposes meet in the one goal, which means that everything that happens is at least fair. 'You have seen all the evil that I [!] brought upon Jerusalem and upon all the cities of Judah. Behold, this day they are a desolation, and no one dwells in them, because of the wickedness that they [!] committed' (Jer.44.2f.) But the catastrophic consequences of such thought are likewise known; for if things go badly for me then I too must be to blame. That is an extremely inhumane solution (John 9.2f.): too many victims are not to blame. For Christians that inevitably had to become clear with the death of Jesus. For if anyone was innocent of his death it was the one who had fulfilled the will of God. With good reason this aporia is resolved in another way: death cannot have the last word, since love is stronger than death (Song of Solomon 8.6). God is and remains faithful (I Cor.1.9), so he did not leave his son in death. This solution too does not describe an objective reality but a limit experience which transcends all human understanding.

Such considerations are alien to Job and his wife.[4] They are victims of robbery, threat and sickness. Bands of thieves and warlike hordes have fallen on them (1.6–20). In their situation they have neither the inspiration nor the strength to cope with scholarly theories. The framework story gives the narrative a dark background which describes the paradoxical situation of the trusting couple. The more we attribute everything to the one creator and governor of the world, the more the faces of God and his adversary are mixed in him. Amos already asked, 'Does evil befall a city, unless Yahweh has done it?' (Amos 3.6). In Job God and his security service find themselves involved in a cruel game. But initially Job reacts submissively:

> The Lord has given, the Lord has taken away,
> Blessed be the name of the Lord (1.21).

This submissiveness only goads the torturer on (2.1–8). However, Job still has reserves of good memory:

> Shall we receive good at the hand of God,
> And shall we not receive evil? (2.10).

All religions attempt to find explanations even in suffering, to trivialize suffering as mere semblance, or to preserve an equilibrium, an ultimate moral order. 'Yahweh has made everything for his purpose, even the wicked for the day of trouble' (Prov.16.4). So are Hitler and the other perpetrators of crimes against humanity God's will? That would mean no less than that not only evil, the experience of pain and suffering in themselves, but also the evil of the heart and the grimness of all destruction can, indeed must, be willed by Yahweh.[5] The prophetic religions in particular are confronted with this question. In the understanding of the Bible belief in creation does not create any concept of God which is innocent and free of conflict, but rather the dramatic clash between on the one hand a boundless hope in God's goodness and on the other the completely hopeless experiences with which the victims of the world are confronted. We know only one hope which, like Abraham, hopes 'despite everything' (Gen.15.16; Rom.4.18). Because Job stakes all on it and nevertheless does not suppress his anger, he has become a topical figure of world literature.[6] Even Job's religious reserves will at one point be exhausted and end in naked despair (3.3):

> Let the day perish wherein I was born,
> And the night which said, 'A man-child is conceived.'

Job experiences God as an enemy (30.21). God's look is burdensome to him (7.19) and God's action has fatal consequences (13.15). Indeed, God leads to death (30.23). God cannot be found anywhere where he should be helping (23.8f.); he remains dumb and uninvolved (30.20). At the same time his remoteness is Job's innermost wish (7.8f.); before God human beings are a nothingness that passes away (14.1–4). Therefore he persists in his innocence (16.17) and perseveres in his way (17.9); however, that gives him no support. His pleas become direct accusations against God (13.3), sharp protest against God. But where shall Job appeal, if not to God and his right? So all standards collapse, the rules of the religious interpretation of the world no longer apply. Job can only go on protesting against God himself, although he is dependent on God. I see the first message of the book of Job as being this destruction of all illusions, in the light of which all questions about God pose themselves afresh.

II. God: cause – legitimation – responsibility

Who is responsible for this situation? The narrative brings three actors on the stage: God, Satan and the group of robbers and aggressors. It is striking that this third group, who after all are the real perpetrators, play no further role in the narrative. As so often in world history the malefactors are made anonymous and presented as forces of fate. There is mention only of 'war' and 'famine', of 'unrest' and 'enemies'. We simply have messengers who have themselves escaped disaster reporting schematically about the natural catastrophes and the perpetrators (1.14, 16, 17, 18).

> The oxen were ploughing
> And the asses feeding beside them;
> And the Sabeans fell upon them and took them,
> And slew the servants with the edge of the sword.

They are fate in the literal sense of the word: neither Job nor the theologians Eliphaz, Bildad and Zophar,[7] whom Job counts his friends, go into them later. Perhaps that is the reason why the story proves so two-edged to our expectations. Job protests and then surrenders, as we shall see in more detail later. Nor is anything more said about Satan. That is a pity, since all religions and cultures have a need to name 'adversaries' or malicious gods, 'devils', 'demons', 'evil powers', forces of destruction or a 'fate', even if they are not said to be entities. But only those who name them can overcome them. Even monotheistic cultures have never completely overcome their dualism between salvation and disaster, because we always experience the world and life as ambiguous. On the contrary, the more we stake all on God, the darker the abyss that breaks open alongside him or in him.

Thus for the story of Job, only God himself remains. He has staged the events; Satan and the villains are completely at his service. He achieves his goal, namely the testing of this pious man. Evidently Job is to realize that he has to fit in with the course of the world and what befalls his own body without saying a word against it and in sober realism. So the book of Job takes up a strikingly modern question. In an enlightened way it excludes intermediate mythical forces. Only God and human beings count: there is no thought about the course of natural forces.

1. Calculating happiness and unhappiness

Thus it seems a matter of course that God himself is responsible for the catastrophe, since no one else can freely control the course of things from a superior position. That is the obvious and appropriate reaction of all those who are beaten and humbled, as is evident from shattering Psalm texts.[8] Belief in the omnipotence of God automatically leads to all the theories that seek to produce the moral equilibrium mentioned above, between human behaviour and human fate. Only in this way can God's action be brought into a comprehensible system. According to the book of Revelation even those who have been slain wait for God's intervention: 'O sovereign Lord, holy and true, how long before you judge and avenge our blood on those who dwell on the earth?' (Rev.6.10). To whom else are they to turn? Who else, as we would put it, is responsible? But what do we mean here by response and responsibility? These abstract concepts are not to be found in the book of Job. They are modern terms, often used today. They became highly significant especially in Christian cultures, in which three important ideas have come together: freedom of decision, legalistic moral accounting and concern, and the obligation of care for fellow human beings and nature.[9] They have become even more significant in the twentieth century, since nature, the environment and society confront us with ever more complex systems which we cannot simply let go in their own confus-ing dynamic. Response and responsibility help us create order and basic orientations. So we want to know simple reasons, and preferably persons, which are 'respon-sible' for an event. They have brought it about, allowed it, not prevented it, or (a favourite in political analyses) brought about long-term conditions which led to the present situation. Of course the quest for someone respon-sible is not always positive, for it often lets us off, though we are also involved, at the wrong time or gives the impression that we can settle all problems by punishing the guilty. That is the concern not of Job, but rather of his friends. They want to comfort him (2.11), but basically they hurt him and make the situation even worse. Eliphaz speaks of human retribution and responsibility (4.1–11), as does Bildad (8.1–7), and after a long prelude and indirectly so does Zophar (11.13–20). The two further rounds of speeches show that these gentlemen can only intensify the painful theme by launching personal attacks (20.4–29). But do we need a theology which in its lack of imagination demonstrates only our wickedness?

> The heavens will reveal his iniquity,
> And the earth will rise up against him.
> The possessions of his house will be carried away,
> Dragged off in the day of God's wrath.
> This is the wicked man's portion from God,
> The heritage decreed for him by God (20.27–29).

This assertion sounds pious, but it is pure ideology, since it is meant in a cynical way: the victims of earthquake and flood are transgressors before God because they are victims. But basically they cannot hold anything concrete against Job. It is their picture of a God who is a moral bookkeeper that leads them to impermissible conclusions, to attacks and insults. This is an image of God which down to the present day is a temptation for monotheistic explanations of the world.

2. Self-righteousness and self-respect

It seems to me that the book of Job is written against this bookkeeping which sets down guilt and responsibility in red figures. Job does not get involved in this reckoning, but rejects it in two ways. First, he shows that the theory of retribution advanced by his opponents does not add up, and can never add up. For 'how can a man be just before God?' (9.2). So no one, not even the best, is guiltless before God. Therefore God can also despise the noble and loosen the belt which gives the strong their power (12.21). Here the argument about retribution is rejected. Secondly, Job increasingly comes up against the hard core of the problem. We may ask: why does Job allow himself to be lured to the question of retribution if it leads in the wrong direction? Isn't he beginning to justify himself against the three men? Isn't he thus becoming self-righteous?

Certainly the drama of the story leads to a vicious circle of defence and new accusations. Job turns the accusations made by his friends against them.

At some point Bildad begins to defend himself. Indeed one could think that he had suffered the fate of Job: 'Why are we counted as cattle? Why are we stupid in your sight?' (18.3). The same is true of Zophar, who equally feels himself insulted (20.3). Here too Eliphaz reacts with a greater understanding than his colleagues in that he extends the horizon of transgressions – so to speak in a critique of society – to Job's earlier position as such. At any rate he is one of the leading merchants and landowners. If need be land will be pledged, others must suffer their poverty, power and possessions are bound up together, his goodness degenerates into favouritism (22.6–9).

How does Job react to these thoughts? Here the texts are clear. At no point does Job praise himself as being righteous. Granted he consistently rejects the conclusion of the three theologians, since none of them can point to any concrete transgression in him. However, he does not react to Eliphaz's comprehensive and fundamental criticism with rejection but with restraint. He calls forth God's own verdict (23.1–17). He himself has done no evil for which he is directly responsible and so he has not caused his misery either. This is an important message for the context of our present: Job maintains his self-contempt even before God. He does not make it a principle and does not display it: complaint and despair come first to his lips (3.1–26). But then he also wants to be clear about his failure: 'If I sin, what do I do to you, you watcher of men? Why have you made me your mark?' (7.20; cf. 6.24; 10.5; 13.23; 27.6; 31.4–34). So he does not want to present himself as a model of innocence; at the same time he wants to be enlightened about his transgression:

Do not condemn me
Let me know
Why you contend against me (10.2; 13.25).

Or at least forgiveness:

Why do you not pardon my transgression
And take away my iniquity (7.21).

Finally, as we shall see, he appeals to God himself.

3. Why?

Job is looking for reasons. Perhaps his misery is compelling him to reorientate himself. So he throws out a set of 'why?' questions. First comes the 'why?' of despair, of retreat, of refusal. 'Why did I not die the moment I came out of my mother's womb?' 'Why does he give light to the wretched?' (3.11, 20; cf.10.18). Then there is the 'why?' of despair at justice: 'Why do the wicked live, reach old age, and grow mighty in power?' (21.7), and why is the expectation that the good will be rewarded and the unjust punished constantly refuted (21.9–34)? It is these questions that sow discord among the pious, because their experiences of life are suddenly so different. The wretched are suddenly regarded as the troublemakers who do not bow to their fates. Bildad feels insulted (18.3), and Job no longer understands his friends: 'Why have you then become altogether vain?' (27.12). God's curse becomes the contempt with which his fellow human beings treat him – in a social system which is collapsing: 'Why do you pursue me like God, why are you not satisfied with my flesh?' (19.22).

There is no difficulty in transferring to the modern world this fragmenting network of codes, values and norms, of self-confidence, interpretations of the world and things that are taken for granted. Precisely the same thing happens today when people are cast into wretchedness, become social outcasts and have to take responsibility for their exceptional situation. This is the crisis that Auschwitz has brought on European theology and which we are only gradually beginning to understand.[10]

But this book remains important for a further reason. Precisely at this point in the story of Job faith in the one God, the creator of the world, becomes effective. This faith does not mean (in the modern scientific sense of the word) that God, the omnipotent, causes everything. Creation, omnipotence and guidance of the world do not mean that God brings about everything so clearly and one-sidedly as it then happens. The complex self-activating systems of which we spoke cannot now be denied either. Faith means an interpretation of the world and includes a remarkably tense attempt: we want to understand world, history and individual destinies from the one mysteriously comprehensive perspective that we call 'God'. Thus 'God' concentrates this endless network of problems into an ultimate and comprehensive question 'why?'. The more open the questions themselves are, the more the burden falls on 'God'. All those who once were or are victims know this situation.

But the operation proposed is dangerous, as the story of Job shows. For imperceptibly not only my existence and the justice of the world enter the discussion, but also the question whether our life and action, our living together, a basic trust in the course of history, make any sense. However, bringing the contrary questions together and constantly confronting them is one of the tasks of faith, and not their radical solution. For this reason the book of Job also sums up broken trust in the world and fellow human beings by putting the question 'why?' to God: 'Why do you not let me die?' (10.18). 'Why do you hide your face and regard me as your enemy?' (13.24). Job complains that this basic question of a collapsing life, threatened by death, is never answered. Faith in the one God does not seek just a synchronous unity of the world, but also a unity of time, which comprises past and future. This makes patience possible, but also creates an urgent impatience: we cannot wait for ever:

> Why are not times of judgment kept by the Almighty,
> And why do those who know him never see his days? (24.1).

4. The sense of responsibility

So is it not God's business to put right the disorder of the world? The more often I read Job's speeches, the more it strikes me in what a differentiated way they are formulated. On the one hand Job is the pious person who will not quickly allow himself to be robbed of trust in God. That finds the full assent of those who trust in God. On the other hand this trust in God cannot simply be translated into one of the theories of justice which are so familiar above all to the writings of the biblical wisdom literature. As we saw above, Job raises questions on *all* sides and faces them, relates them to his own situation. He does not want answers which simply excuse him (or God). So he breaks through the alternatives posed by his theological friends which can still be heard today. This too meets with the assent of many of us. Evidently he wants quite simply, but in complete honesty, to discover the conditions which determine his fate. But what are these conditions?

At this point for Job, as for all those who suffer, who are scorned and outcasts, the problem become acute. These open questions do not clarify but confuse. They reflect the deep existential disorientation of people who do not want to submit blindly to their fate. Certainly Job experiences God as his enemy, but at the same time he does not make him responsible for his fate. Certainly Job makes his wife face the fact that his life (whatever it may be) is now ended (2.9), nevertheless he grapples with his fate. Certainly he denies the theologians his friendship, because they are only deceiving him (21.34); nevertheless he continues to engage in question and answer with them. The decisive change takes place after the first round of his friends' speeches. They have robbed him of all his arguments. But what do they know of the circumstances, of God himself whom they seem to know? Job knows as much (or as little) as his opponents about God's power (12.7–24). With what right then must those who call on God be mocked (12.4)? Therefore Job breaks through a boundary which is deeply rooted in Jewish but also in Christian and Muslim tradition. He denies his friends the right to speak in the name of God (13.7). After Job has called on God, he wants an answer from God himself (12.4). He wants to defend his ways before God (13.5), to hear from God what he has done wrong (13.23).

> Then call, and I will answer;
> Or let me speak, and reply to me (13.22).

But against what God is Job protesting, and from whom is he requiring an answer? Soon it proves that for Job the image of God itself is splitting, for now he has no alternative than to call to his defence the God whom he experiences as his enemy. He appeals to a better God. He requires – over and above anything that is usual in religion – a direct guarantee: 'Lay down a pledge with me for yourself' (17.3). In a kind of utopian anticipation of a last judgment here is the hopeful appeal to God against God. 'Even now, behold my witness is in heaven, and he that vouches for me is on high' (16.19). We hear no more of this 'guarantor' that could be connected with our knowledge of God, but this shows the God of the theologians his limits. Deeply provoked and in ultimate self-contempt, at the same time Job cries out:

> For I know that my Redeemer lives
> And an advocate will raise me from the dust.
> Even after my skin has been destroyed,
> And my flesh torn from me,
> I will see God.
> That you may know that there is a judgment (19.25, 26, 29c).

With this extreme attempt Job puts his existence, his self-contempt, himself, at stake. The conclusion is usually that Job is protesting against God, that he is making God responsible. But 'responsible' primarily means just 'giving a response': no less, but also no more. Those who have been humiliated pose questions and quite obviously they have a right to do so. In a world which is becoming increasingly complicated (and about whose inner diversity we are discovering more and more), questions are posed to many agents and systems, to society and politics, to science and medicine, to biographies and history, to individual action, our own and that of others. But the less they can explain my concrete fate, the more faith directs a comprehensive question to God:

> O that I had one to hear me! (31.35).

Here they would not be declaring God to be the cause of our misery (even Job does not do that), but especially in misery they want to be heard, they cry to him, they ask him for help, they hope for justice and a last orientation from him. If God is responsible for the course of the world, then that means primarily that a God of goodness and power must put these questions to himself. However, those who complain and cry out (if they trust in God) are also ready to involve their own existence in this play of question and 'responsibility' to the point that they no longer have anything to lose. The answers will then transcend the levels of pure information and explanation, for what else would God reveal to them than something unexpected which changes their very existence?

The book of Job helps us to understand such 'responsibility' in a new and elementary way. Of course we know that we cannot reduce the problem of responsibility to the question of a one-sided causation. With 'responsibility' we evaluate complex conditions and emphasizing their significance. We attribute them to particular people or authorities.[11] The notion of freedom lives on this notion of calculable responsibility. So they have in common an important function of orientation – the serious consequence of a prophetic heritage. This also includes the fact that in solidarity (or even as voluntary representatives) we take over the fates of other people, and at least can make ourselves responsible for changing them. So it would be absurd to answer that God, who bears ultimate responsibility, willed or caused concrete misery. But if God 'creates' the world and human beings, says a quiet basic 'yes' to them, and thus if God accepts us human beings as his image and likeness (Gen.1.26), then we want at least to know about the other side of this comprehensive love and affirmation, what it costs us or (as the New Testament says), at what price we have been bought (I Cor.6.20). Precisely because Job has understood the depth and radical nature of such responsibility, he grows beyond individual questions, for he discovers his own contradictions in God and vice versa. Only God himself can respond to them. So God is not evading his responsibility in concealing causal chains or burdening the wretched with guilt, but is absent by withdrawing himself. The cry falls silent in the void:

> I would learn what he would answer me,
> And understand what he says to me.
> Would he contend with me in the greatness of his power?
> No, he would give heed to me.
> Behold I go eastward, and he is not there,
> westward and I cannot perceive him,

northward I do not perceive his action,
if I turn southward, I do not see him (23.5–6, 8–9).

So how is it possible for God to withdraw from this world as it is? How can
he allow all the misery, pain and poverty the appearance of a last confirmation? How is it possible that even God's messengers, the religions and their
theologies, keep giving abbreviated answers? That is the basic question
which is concealed by this accusation of God: where is the God who does not
show himself in particular to the wretched?[12]

III. Hearing and seeing

Sometimes a distinction is made between cultures of shame and cultures
of guilt.[13] This distinction has not been generally recognized, but quite
certainly the question of personal accountability, responsibility and guilt
plays a dominant role in the prophetic cultures (of Judaism, Christianity and
Islam). Here something important is often forgotten: experiences of shame
precede questions of responsibility. The question of our guilt and God's
guilt is one thing; the question whether we can still allow ourselves to be seen
before God and human beings, whether God will still let us see him, is
another. That is extremely important for our relationship to God.

1. Face and heart

There is an interesting linguistic dualism in Egyptian religious writings.[14]
The relationship of one human being to another is expressed with two
supplementary metaphors. We bear things 'in the heart' or something
appears to me 'in the face'.

I bear others' opinions of me 'in the heart'. I consider what they think
about me, what they say, what I hear. From that I draw my conclusions
about justice or guilt. This is not a direct experience but the assessment of
my (past) action; I am made responsible for that. This sphere of perception
in the heart is governed by speaking and hearing;[15] past and memory are the
medium of discussion. The whole controversy which the book of Job has
presented to us so far is played out at this level, the level of the word. But at
the end, Job shows us that in the absence of God this reflection, the discussion of freedom and guilt, ultimately does not lead to any solution: that is the
fate of the classical problem of theodicy.[16] Who in the Christian tradition
knew this better than Paul, who denies us all justification by our own works
(Rom.3–4)?

As if the God of the book of Job were only waiting for this insight, he now appears, once the discussion between Job and his friends has come to grief.[17] Now the absent one speaks 'from the storm'. Imagine a hurricane which is difficult to withstand in the wilderness (28.1). God is now present, fully present, in the power of this natural phenomenon (38–41). The tone changes; three perspectives now govern the atmosphere: 1. God himself speaks in exaltation and superiority, time and again, of himself; he alone defines the theme. That in particular creates the experience that God is now dominating the scene. No one needs any longer to speak of him at this moment. He can be seen in his power. Attention is directed to *God himself.* 2. God shows Job the miracle of creation. The 'only' important thing is the glory that he shows, including the hippopotamus and the crocodile (38f.; 40.14–41.26). So attention is directed to *reality*. 3. In short, with biting irony God points out to Job his limitations (40.71–3). The situation of *Job* no longer plays a role.

How is God's answer to be understood? Why does God now appears as the almighty, and why is Job now so humiliated before God, although he was so clearly concerned for God's dignity? Does not hope in a God who gives the dishonoured their due collapse? In face we must ask ourselves whether our 'modern' interpretations of God which are so strongly concerned with human dignity and loftiness do justice to the message of the book of Job? I am afraid that we are no longer bringing God and our world into a really religious relationship. For many of us God is up there, far from us, as absent as he was from the talk of the three friends. God is at most still in a position to guide the world and intervene among human beings – against their will. That is the one-sided view of a reflecting 'heart' which no longer sees God because it has lost 'sight' of God.

But the book of Job introduces the dimension of this 'face' again in a dramatic way. God, the absent one, is now unexpectedly present. He 'appears', as some translations of the book of Job put it. He, God himself, does not invite Job to reflect but almost compels Job to see him, to look into him. This is a direct, so to speak unreflected, perception which precedes all consideration. The immediate feeling of shame, hope for honour, fear of shame, belongs in this sphere of experience. If I feel uncovered by this God, affected in my identity, do I feel that I belong and am desired? This level of 'inter-vision' knows no veils. It no longer allows any immunizing reflection. The eyes of Adam and Eve were opened, they recognized that they were stripped bare, naked (Gen.3.7). Isaiah sees Yahweh on his throne, whereupon he cries out, 'Woe is me, I am lost' (6.5). In the book of Revelation we see 'a new heaven and a new earth' (Rev.21.1). This overwhelming presence, this unprotected standing before God, is of central importance in all religions.[18] We could describe religion as an experiential action in which all relations of time are overcome and sublated into the absolute presence. Talk about God goes over into addressing God. Therefore the question of God, if it is posed authentically and God is really good, always issues in this 'over against' and 'now' which can be seen and experienced. As we also we ask about God and our own responsibility, this question issues in the dimension of the present. How I stand with you, God, here and now? How do you show yourself to me? In the light of this condition of the world, in the light of my wretchedness (and now that I have become ridiculous with my questions) are you full of honour or are you yourself ridiculous in the face of this world? Do you show yourself to my eyes as powerful or small, as meaningless and fundamentally insignificant?[19] Can the heavens really praise you (Ps.19.2)?

2. *Ever new questions*

I am afraid that we in Western culture have lost this dimension of a vital, almost physical, experience of God. I also suggest that far too often we call God to account as false reasons and with superficial arguments. He 'puts his hand on his mouth' (40.5) and 'refutes' (42.6). In his wretchedness Job had to relearn his faith, which meant a radical existential conversion. Job's friends are not justified here, but – together with Job – even more radically refuted. Is that the whole story? Certainly real trust in God requires of us the readiness to long to choose ourselves as the perspective on life. Nevertheless I do not dare to offer this answer of the book of Job to the poorest of the poor, the victims of the Shoah or the genocide in Rwanda, the socially devastated in the many economically dependent countries, because only God can show himself in this way.

God has taught Job to turn his gaze to the reality of this world. Today this includes the enormous significance of cultural, social, political and economic dimensions. The children of the era of globalization also need to learn from God to take these dimensions seriously – and to react to them. But must there not also be a last and saving responsibility for the present state of the world? Indeed this responsibility involves men and women being brothers and sisters to one another. The cry to God finds an answer only in a world in which God's solidarity with us itself becomes reality. Only those who understand the cry to God as a concrete 'option for the poor' can recognize the beginning of an answer.[20]

The answers given here are not new, but they always need to be rediscovered. The book of Job is not a textbook but a script for learning God's presence and the readiness to allow oneself to be addressed by him. At the same time it tells us the true history of the humiliated among us and those who have been deprived of their rights. It is an authentic, abiding *theatrum mundi* which also constantly repeats itself in the future,[21] and shows us how God presents responsibility to us.

Translated by John Bowden

Notes

1. H. Häring, *Das Böse in der Welt. Gottes Macht oder Ohnmacht?*, Darmstadt 1999, pp. 15–36.

2. '*Id quod nocet*': *De moribus Manichaeorum* II, 3, 5 (PL 32,1346), vgl. Häring (n.1), pp. 3–6.

3. K. Barth. 'God and Nothingness', *Churh Dogmatics* III/3, Edinburgh 1961, pp. 289–368.

4. This article has been inspired by a marvellous book by E. van Wolde, *Mr and Mrs Job*, London 1997.

5. W. Gross und K.-J. Kuschel, '*Ich schaffe Finsternis und Unheil.*' *Ist Gott verantwortlich für das Übel?*, Mainz 1992.

6. G. Langenhorst, *Hiob. Unser Zeitgenosse. Die literarische Hiob-Rezeption im 20. Jahrhundert als theologische Herausforderung*, Mainz ²1995.

7. I shall not comment here on the four speeches by Elihu (32.1–37.24), which have not been woven into the overall text editorially, but have clearly been inserted *en bloc*.

8. This drama has been presented very vividly in an exegesis of Ps. 88 by U. Berges, *Schweigen ist Silber – Klagen ist Gold. Das Drama der Gottesbeziehung aus alttestamentlicher Sicht mit einer Auslegung zu Ps 88*, Münster 2003. Further important literature on the problem is mentioned there.

9. H. Jonas, *Das Prinzip Verantwortung*, Frankfurt 1979; A. Etzioni, *Die Verantwortungsgesellschaft*, Frankfurt 1997.

10. R. Ammicht-Quinn, *Von Lissabon nach Auschwitz. Zum Paradigmenwechsel der Theodizeefrage*, Freiburg 1992.

11. P. Ricoeur, *Finitude en Culpabilité I. L'homme faillible*, Paris 1960.

12. The question of the presence of God is not just a twentieth-century one. As early as 1512 the painter Matthias Grünewald makes Antony, tempted by demons, say: '*Ubi eras bone Ihesu, ubi eras? Quare non affuisti ut sanares vulnera mea?*' [Where were you, good Jesus, where were you? Why did you not come to heal my wounds?] (Isenheim altar, Colmar, France).

13. T. Schirrmacher, 'Scham- und Schuldkultur', *Querschnitte* 14. 7, July 2001.

14. J. Assmann, *Herrschaft und Heil. Politische Theologie in Altägypten, Israel und Europa*, Munich 2000, pp. 133–7.

15. Assmann calls this the sphere of 'interlocution'. H. W. Wolff, *Anthropology of*

the *Old Testament*, Philadelphia 1974; J. Assmann (ed.), *Die Erfindung des inneren Menschen*, Gütersloh 1993, pp. 81–113. Unfortunately the classical Catholic devotion to the Sacred Heart of Jesus has not made any connection with the dimensions mentioned.

16. A. Kreiner, *Gott im Leid. Zur Stichhaltigkeit der Theodizee-Argumente*, Freiburg 1997.

17. Y. Pyeon, *You Have Not Spoken What Is Right About Me. Intertextuality and the Book of Job*, New York 2003.

18. G. H. Seidler, *Der Blick des Andern*, Stuttgart 1995. From this perspective intensive attention still needs to be paid to the work of E. Lévinas.

19. This differentiation could help to work out the dilemma of the classical question of theodicy. This is probably also the reason why we expect help from intercessory prayer but do not lose our trust in God when it does not come. The decisive question is: can we trust God in prayer and so to speak hand ourselves over to him completely? In this way do we succeed in understanding reality as it really is?

20. E. Schillebeeckx, *Jesus. An Experiment in Christology*, London and New York 1974, pp. 612–25.

21. G. Theobald, *Hiobs Botschaft. Die Ablösung der metaphysischen durch die poetische Theodizee*, Gütersloh 1983.

'Neither Punishment nor Reward': Divine Gratuitousness and Moral Order

JAN JANS

That the heavens belong to the Lord will hardly be disputed by any of the traditions of theism. However, what are the implications for the 'moral order' following from the claim that by divine gratuitousness, the earth is truly the realm of human responsibility? In this article, I will first explore whether what looks like the classical paradigm in which God is perceived as (some ultimate) judge can be deconstructed under the impulse of an understanding of divine gratuitousness. Next, I venture into a reconstruction of divine covenant and moral order by asking about the proper relationship between grace and ethics. Finally, I suggest a way of dealing with some objections against such a reconstruction by probing the inner dynamics within a morality which understands itself as at the same time human(e) and divine.

I. Exploring a paradigm shift

If experience can be trusted, the context and the meaning of the neologism 'god-mode' might not be immediately evident to the large majority of people committed to faith, theology and ethics. I encountered this 'god-mode' while researching some of the ethical questions arising within the field of ICT – Information and Communication Technology.[1] Looking into the set-up and functioning of computer games simulating all kinds of battle – also known as 'shoot-them-up' – I came across the phenomenon of the 'cheat-mode'. A cheat-mode is a function of the game that can be activated by the player when he [sic] isn't making enough progress and/or if he is on the brink of being defeated by the enemies unleashed by the game. The ultimate version of such a cheat-mode by which a player acquires unlimited resources such as armour and ammunition but also immortality and especially 'the power to utterly destroy any enemy at will' is dubbed the 'god-mode', because it is achieved after entering a command line such as 'I am god'.[2]

Of course, it would be easy simply to shrug one's shoulders and dismiss this as an outstanding example of the secular abuse of religious terminology. However, it might be more then just an intuition that this peculiar 'god-talk' and its associated attributes do have deep roots in religious culture and resonate with peculiar images of the divine from which these violent and destructive understandings arise. I think that these roots are very close to the reason why many comprehensive or all-risks insurance policies still exclude so-called 'acts of God' – usually understood as natural disasters – both because of their sheer magnitude and especially because of their seeming arbitrariness.

Next, I would like to suggest that this notion of 'seeming' arbitrariness opens the door to one of the most vexing fundamental problems that surfaces time and again whenever the effort is made to relate 'moral order' and 'the realm of the divine'. In Greco-Western moral philosophy, this problem is well known as 'The Euthyphro Dilemma' or, in more general terms as 'Divine Command Theory'.[3] This theory holds that the moral obligations of human beings rest on the divine commands of the gods simply and solely because the gods impose them. In the discussion between Euthyphro and Socrates, Plato assigns the defence of this position to Euthyphro: whatever our human(e) feelings and experiences are, the sole and final criteria for morality are the divine commandments, which even if they appear to be arbitrary require unconditional obedience. Conversely, the position of Socrates is that there is a standard for morality which is independent of the gods and which can even be used to assay divine commandments.[4] (At the same time this opens up the possibility of paying obedience to the gods, not because their commandments are absolute on the basis of their power or divine will, but because the commandments correspond with the good and are understood to be issued for precisely that very reason.)

However, the different epistemological presuppositions of both positions have grave consequences. Euthyphro's normative voluntarism on the one hand leads to parity between the divine laws issued by gods and morality, thus rendering any practical reflection on their moral content superfluous and criticism even impossible. At most, the question remains how humans can 'know with certainty' what the divine commandments are. Socrates' normative realism on the other hand is at the same time the beginnings of reflection on the content and critical evaluation of factual ethics – even in the form of commandments issued by gods – because the true good can be assayed by the standard of ethics, which is nothing but human flourishing. This also means that both positions are incompatible in their fundamental idea of morality. The first position will sweep aside as totally absurd some assessment of divine arbitrariness or im/morality because morality itself is nothing but blind obedience to a divine command without any other or further point of reference. The core of the second position, however, consists in situating ethics as bound to goodness to which not just humans but also even the gods should owe obedience.

In view of such incompatibility, one might be surprised that 'divine command theory' attracts any support at all. Its attraction, I would suggest, lies in the connection that it allows between on the one hand moral behaviour the content of which is given by the divine commandments, and on the other some kind of reward, but especially punishment. The connection is attractive because of its ultimate guarantee: no single mortal can escape divine judgment and therefore both the seriousness of moral behaviour and actual and/or final justice appear to be substantiated. The connection is also attractive because it seems to team up very well with biblical images and stories of divine reward and punishment as the result of human obedience or transgression.

Indeed, it is not at all bad to paint a bleak picture of the inevitability of God's judgment in terms of punishment. In the logic of creation-redemption-eschatology, the very *felix culpa* that triggers the whole of the economy of salvation is also the curse of sin that from the very origin on casts a shadow on morality and seems to allow for a theology that entertains inescapable predestination and the acceptance of a *massa damnata*.[5] But even the reassurance that in the end divine justice will prevail or the equally strong conviction that there is a necessary connection between concrete evil and misbehaviour is hardly a plausible reply to the existential reality of suffering through which one is tempted to mix up images of a gracious God and a deceiving Satan. Job's refusal to give in to this temptation at least hints at an alternative vision in which the divine is conceived to relate to morality not by a retributive justice of reward and punishment but by gratuitousness. It is such an alternative vision that may open our eyes to the original sin of avoiding responsibility by cheaply blaming us or someone else – as in the paradigmatic case of the male blaming the female and the female blaming the serpent – and thereby giving up responsible freedom as the core of our own dignity.[6] Furthermore, such an alternative vision of gratuitousness allows for reflection on the relation between the divine and morality not in the usual terms of imposed 'commandments' and a concomitant imposed obedience, but in terms of 'covenant', inviting the perspective of response and participation. It is this paradigm that I would like to explore in the second section of this article.

II. Morality and divine covenant

My first point is to highlight the crucial difference between the gods who officiate in whatever divine command theory and the biblical suggestion that the hidden God of the covenant is revealed through the struggle for human flourishing.[7] The gods of the pantheon see no difficulty in trespassing even their own rules of morality if this suits them, regardless of the consequences, but the God of the covenant is faithful to the moral order of the promise made. Of course, it is very easy – abundantly even on the basis of the scriptural account about the liberation from slavery and the occupation of the promised land – to picture this God as the Lord of the mighty hand and awesome signs; at the same time this offers a 'divine' justification for some of the atrocities recounted. How difficult it can be really to deal with this interpretation of a divinely substantiated moral order is demonstrated by a passage from the famous 'confession of guilt' of the Roman Catholic Church issued in December 1999:

> ... acts of violence perpetrated by Israel against other peoples, which would seem to require a request for forgiveness from those people or from their descendants, are understood to be the execution of divine directives, as for example *Gn* [sic: *Josh*] 2–11 and *Dt* 7:2 (the extermination of the Canaanites), or 1 *Sm* 15 and *Dt* 25:19 (the destruction of the Amalekites). In such cases, the involvement of a divine command would seem to exclude any possible request for forgiveness.

The accompanying note 36 explains:

> Cf. the analogous case of the repudiation of foreign wives described in *Ezr* 9–10, with all the negative consequences which this would have had for these women. The question of a request for forgiveness addressed to them (and/or to their descendents) is not treated, since their repudiation is presented as a requirement of God's law (cf. *Dt* 7:3) in all these chapters.[8]

Next, my reading of the divine covenant aimed at salvation would dispute such interpretations and point instead to a more fundamental and internal dynamic within this covenant between the gratuitous divine desire for and delight in goodness – grace – and the proper way in which human beings deal with each other – ethics. In this reading, an inexhaustible ethical dynamism begins with the very name of God revealed to Moses in Exodus 3.14 – a name that turns out to be a verb: 'I am who is.' The context of this name is the response of YHWH to the lamentations of the oppressed, a response the content of which is to bring about liberation. Not surprisingly, this very context is again recalled in the passages further down in Exodus and also in Deuteronomy that are known as 'The Decalogue' or 'The Ten Commandments' as paradigmatic summaries of the human(e) response to God's grace. For the record: the extent to which a morality of imposed commandments has permeated liturgy and catechesis can very well be illustrated in the leaving out of this 'context of liberation' in the so-called catechetical formulations of the Ten Commandments in which the inner interaction between God's initiative – grace – and the response of human beings – ethics – has been lost sight of.[9]

In focusing on this dynamic, I would suggest that we also gain a better understanding of the meaning of this 'context of liberation' as triggering self-criticism within the realm of an ethics understanding itself as a response to divine grace. Again, against the horizon of the discussion between Socrates and Euthyphro, one could think of the relation between salvation and ethics as 'straightforward': one carries out the will of God because of the reward that follows from such obedience and/or especially to evade the punishment that one brings upon oneself through disobedience. And indeed, such an interpretation can claim biblical support from within the Decalogue itself: '. . . I the LORD your God am a jealous God, punishing children for the iniquity of parents, to the third and fourth generation of those who reject me, but showing steadfast love to the thousandth generation of those who love me and keep my commandments' (Deut.5.9–10; cf. Ex.20.5–6).[10]

Nevertheless, the relation between divine salvation and a corresponding ethics can also be thought of as 'intrinsic': the very content of the values and norms as they are practically lived out are then nothing but the actual and concrete mediation of this salvation. This means that they are the rules and agreements that provide the framework to make the step from mere survival towards living together well, and as such function as the returning touchstone for any further particular normative discourse. But – and this is the ethical self-criticism to which I alluded above – should such a reading not also apply with regard to the formulation and interpretation of the 'divine' moral order itself? I think that the answer to this question is affirmative and would like to illustrate this with two biblical examples.

The first example is the shift in the content of the 'tenth commandment' between its formulations in Exodus and Deuteronomy. Exodus 20.17 reads as follows: 'You shall not covet your neighbour's house; you shall not covet your neighbour's wife, or male or female slave, or ox, or donkey, or anything that belongs to your neighbour.' Deuteronomy 5.21 states: 'Neither shall you covet your neighbour's wife. Neither shall you desire your neighbour's house, or field, or male or female slave, or ox or donkey, or anything that belongs to your neighbour.' The shift is remarkable because in the first and earlier text the neighbour's wife is named following the house, including her as part of the properties belonging to her husband, whereas in the second, later, formulation the commandment is now a diptych in which the neighbour's wife comes first, followed by a description of what kind of things belong to 'the house'. Of course, such a shift could be very easily explained (away) by the followers of Euthyphro, who would just have to point to God's voluntarism whereby the divine will simply equals the moral law. In contrast to this approach, I would suggest that we have to pay attention to the content of the shift, which from the ethical point of view is not just a change but a real improvement for both the neighbour and his wife. However, let us for a moment speculate that the author of Deuteronomy was confronted with a reproach such as: 'it is all very well that the relation between a neighbour and his wife is more ethical if she is not counted directly as part of his property; however, this is how the divine order demands it . . .' – a reproach to which the answer might have been: 'Indeed, that is the way it was laid down in writing, but the spirit of a gratuitous God who is aiming at the well-being and liberation of humans calls me to improve on the letter, because divine law should be nothing but the mirror of divine grace.'[11] Therefore, Deuteronomy can rightfully claim – not despite but precisely because of this change/improvement – to present its reading as in accord with our understanding of 'divine' moral order.[12]

If this is true, it demonstrates the reciprocal relation between the context and the content of 'divine commandments' by which the experience gained from actual ethical behaviour constitutively flows back in the understanding of one's proper response to God. Or, in other words: really to obey *God* does not consist in accepting a situation like that in the (Dutch) proverb: 'After the word of God, the brain is locked up,' but is the response of human persons to the invitation to understand the dynamics of ethics as what constitutes a moral order consonant with divine gratuitousness.

The second example is the way in which in all four Gospels Jesus seemingly comes into conflict with the great commandment to keep the sabbath. In Mark 2.23–28 this happens through a discussion on plucking heads of grain on the sabbath, followed by Mark 3.1–5 about healing with a direct reference to the ethical notions 'to do good or to do harm on the sabbath, to save life or to kill' (3.4); in Matthew 1.1–13 similar discussions are narrated; Luke 6.1–10 contains a repetition of these two issues, but there are also Luke 13.10–17 and Luke 14.1–6 with other discussions on healing;

John 9.1–38 again has a story about healing. Now my point here is not the diversity and the narrative richness contained in these passages but the fundamental attitude that shines forth from the behaviour of Jesus and/or the disciples. Mark summarizes this attitude succinctly: 'The sabbath was made for humankind, and not humankind for the sabbath' (2.27). The importance of this for my thesis about the relation between divine moral requirements and ethical behaviour is given further relief if one recalls the massive theological substantiation of the commandment to keep the sabbath in both versions of the Decalogue: in Deut. 5.12–15 with a direct reference to God's salvation out of slavery and in Ex. 20.8–11 by the reference to God's universal work of creation and the built-in rhythm of six days of work but resting on the seventh day. Nevertheless, also this – indeed precisely this – commandment is ethically qualified by Jesus: in the concrete situation in which people find themselves the meaning and significance of such divine morality surfaces by which it can be fulfilled according to the spirit present in it.

III. Human(e) and/or divine morality?

By way of conclusion: to what degree is an ethic which follows the lines above also theology? Or, to put it another way: does not such an approach lead to a reduction of the response towards divine gratuitousness to human(e) responsibility? Furthermore, does not the criticism of reward and punishment as characteristic of divine involvement with human behaviour open up the floodgates to relativism and even indifference?

In partial answer to these objections, I begin by consulting three contemporary moral theologians who in brief but profound statements spell out their vision of the proper relationship between biblical faith and ethics. The first of these definitions is by the Scottish moral theologian John Mahoney and is taken from his 1987 study on the development of moral theology: '[M]oral theology is faith (in God) seeking expression in behaviour.'[13] I notice here an echo from the Letter of James 2.14–26 with its ringing conclusion: 'For just as the body without the spirit is dead, so faith without works is also dead.' The second definition is by the German moral theologian Klaus Demmer, and is taken from his 1989 synthesis article on the self-understanding of theological ethics: 'Moral theology is the scientific study of God's salvific action on behalf of humanity, which in its significance for the ethical behaviour of human beings is hermeneutically systematized and argumentatively presented.'[14] Here I notice the importance of God's gracious initiative and the connection with the full breadth of ethics. The third definition is by the Flemish moral theologian Louis Janssens and is taken from his last publication in 1999, two years before his death: 'It is the task of moral theology to explain how, according to our Christian revelation, our relation to God affects all our doings.'[15] What is important here is the counterpart of the movement stressed by Demmer, namely the accent on the significance of the faith response by humans. The global result of this consultation is to strengthen my earlier rejection of the gods of the pantheon because their voluntaristic stance is incompatible with any vocational ethics. Moreover it does not allow for any representation of God and humanity as moral competitors because of the 'analogy of being' that both connects and differentiates the divine and creation. It also brings me to ask how 'faith', 'salvific action' and 'revelation' qualify each other with regard to their content. If God's revelation *is* salvific action, and faith the response of human persons by which they participate in this realm of grace, then I would venture to say that wherever love and justice are practised, the promise of divine grace and salvation is actualized.[16]

Furthermore, and more directly dealing with (moral) relativism or (religious) indifferentism, the answer does not seem to lie in the assertion 'If God does not exist, everything is permitted', because the background is again a notion of moral behaviour in which the checks and balances are put into place and guarded by a divine judge. Another (Dutch) proverb is illustrative of this position by claiming 'God is watching me – no cursing here!' Now this does not mean that an alternative to such a divine big brother gives up on normativity and the seriousness of ethics; the claim is only that it can do without an external or additional judgment. Somewhat counter-intuitively, I would suggest that the so-called 'Last Judgment' (Matt. 25.31–46) could be an inspiration for such a position because of its apparent 'a-theism' in both the acts mentioned and the intentions of the actors. To inherit the kingdom prepared from the foundation of the world it turns out to be sufficient to feed the hungry and quench the thirsty, to welcome the stranger, to dress the naked, to take care of the sick and to visit the prisoners. Also, this morality is anonymous *and* gratuitous on two counts: those who do the right thing are unaware of the revealed meaning within the goodness they practised, and apparently the Son of Man is not revealed to them in the least of the members of his family. Maybe one could say that Matthew spoils part of this to the degree that those who engage in the 'works of charity' can now be tempted to stray away from 'ethics for ethics' sake' and focus on ending up in eternal life with the righteous on the right-hand side.

The list given by Matthew is clearly neither comprehensive – no doubt, one could add the peacemakers and all those who are persecuted for righteousness' sake – nor is it suggested that each and every one of these good deeds is required. This might shed some light on the place of eternal fire and punishment prepared at the left-hand side of the king. For is it possible to imagine a life worthy of 'moral judgment' without one single act just for goodness' sake on behalf of one of the least? Maybe the 'eternal fire prepared for the devil and his angels' remains empty. And maybe this could very well be the core of the inner connection between divine gratuitousness and any *moral* order.

Notes

1. Cf. Jan Jans, 'Dealing with Virtual Janus. Some Cornerstones for the Teaching of Computer Ethics at School', in *FINE 2001* (Proceedings), ed. Mitsugu Ochi and Masashi Tsuboi, Hiroshima 2001, pp. 49–58; id., 'E-vangelization. A theological reflection on the relation between the internet and Christian Faith', *Bulletin ET* 13, 2002, pp. 59–65 (reprinted in *St Augustine Papers* 2, 2001/1, pp. 25–32).
2. Cf. for example the website http://www.cheatnow.nl, sporting the slogan 'Play God, Cheat Now!'.
3. Cf. Mark Timmons, *Moral Theory: An Introduction*, Lanham 2002, pp. 23–35.
4. Plato, *Euthyphro*, 6d–16a; 10a: 'Socrates: Perhaps we shall learn better, my friend. For consider: is the holy loved by the gods because it is holy? Or is it holy because it is loved by the gods?,' in *Plato's 'Euthyphro' and the earlier theory of forms*, ed. R. E. Allen, London 1970, p. 39.
5. Cf. *Original Sin: A Code of Fallibility*, *Concilium* 2004/1.
6. This connection between responsible freedom and human dignity is spelt out by the Second Vatican Council in its Declaration on Religious Freedom, *Dignitatis humanae* 1–2.
7. I owe the core of this thought to Theo Beemer: 'The struggle against evil, against the robbery of indebted good, and in favour of the birthright of the destitute is a mystagogy, an initiation into God's mystery.' Cf. Theo Beemer, 'Het geboorterecht van de berooiden en de verborgen God', in *Om het geheim van God. Moraaltheologie in de jaren negentig*, ed. Rinus Houdijk, Heerlen 1993, p. 96.
8. Cf. International Theological Commission, *Memory and Reconciliation: the Church and the Faults of the Past*, section 2.1. (http://www.vatican.va/roman_curia/congregations/cfaith/cti_documents/rc_con_cfaith_doc_20000307_memory-reconc-itc_en.html)
9. A striking example is the way in which the *Catechism of the Catholic Church*, in the pages preceding its teaching on the Ten Commandments (nos. 2052–2557), simply presents the biblical accounts and the catechetical formulation side by side. Of course, this abbreviated version is easy to learn by heart but it comes close to the voluntaristic 'why? – just because!' in which obedience itself becomes a trait of ethical virtue.

10. The biblical quotations are taken from the New Revised Standard Version (NRSV).

11. Cf. Karl-Wilhelm Merks, 'Göttliches Recht, menschliches Recht, Menschenrechte. Die Menschlichkeit des "ius divinum"', *Bijdragen* 65, 2004 – forthcoming.

12. Sadly, I have to add that this ethical dynamism needed many more centuries before the ethical truth dawned that also 'male or female slave' are both figuratively and literally untenable.

13. John Mahoney, *The Making of Moral Theology. A Study of the Roman Catholic Tradition*, Oxford 1987, p. 340.

14. Klaus Demmer, 'Das Selbstverständnis der Moraltheologie', in *Grundlagen und Probleme der heutigen Moraltheologie*, ed. Wilhelm Ernst, Würzburg 1989, p. 10. The full quotation is: 'Moral theology is the scientific study of God's salvific action on behalf of humanity, which in its significance for the ethical behaviour of human beings is hermeneutically systematized and argumentatively presented. Moral theology is a theory of action. Historical fulfilment of the history of salvation in Jesus Christ and the still standing promise of eschatological completion are in the same way constitutive for the moral theological discourse. On this foundation a double argument is built: in its orientation towards the faithful, moral theology strives to inquire into the full richness of the given possibilities of being and acting in Jesus Christ; in its orientation towards non-believers, moral theology is directed by the concern not to disrupt the connection with the general ethical dialogue. Each of these phases is correlated to the other.'

15. Louis Janssens, 'Particular Goods and Personalist Morals', in *Ethical Perspectives* (Journal of the European Ethics Network) 6.1, 1999, pp. 55–6.

16. Of course this does not favour any reductionism with regard to ethics and the realm of the divine. On the contrary, any foundation of ethics remains incomplete – and thereby substandard from the human(e) point of view – without the (critical) inclusion of the component of religious practice. Cf. Jan Jans, 'The Fish and Their Water – Implications of Anthropology as the Foundation of Ethics', in *The Sources of Public Morality – On the 'Ethics and Religion' Debate*, Societas Ethica Jahresbericht/Annual 2001, Aarhus 2002, pp. 253–8.

III. Job: Questions around the World

Divine Interventions in Tolkien's Universe

RON PIRSON

'. . . it is not our part to master all the tides of the world, but to do what is in us for the succour of those years wherein we are set, uprooting the evil in the fields that we know, so that those who live after may have clean earth to till. What weather they shall have is not ours to rule.'[1]

Like our universe, the universe created by the English scholar and novelist J.R.R. Tolkien is characterized by a gradual expansion. Unlike ours, it did not start with a 'big bang', nor will it end in a 'big crack' or continue to expand infinitely. Tolkien's creation came into existence during his period of recovery and convalescence after trench fever, which he caught when he was serving his country at the Battle of the Somme in 1917.[2] The development of Tolkien's world came to an end in 1973, when its creator died at the age of 81.

Tolkien's star started shining brightly from the second half of the 1960s onwards, after *The Lord of the Rings* was published as a paperback. His quest of the Ring became a cult book: on university campuses in the United States one could read graffiti like 'Frodo lives' and 'Gandalf for President'. During the last quarter of the twentieth century, *The Lord of the Rings* remained a book that attracted a lot of readers. It was chosen 'book of the century' in England in several polls.[3] Since 2001 the book has gained even more popularity because of the New Zealand director Peter Jackson's adaptation of it for the big screen – which he did quite successfully, as is attested by both the enormous audience figures and the fact that the third part was awarded eleven Oscars in February 2004.

One of the questions to be addressed in this article is: Where in *The Lord of the Rings* does the reader get a notion of the divine, or of the divine order that may lie beyond the physical world – if there is any such notion at all? How does the divine order relate to the physical world, and perhaps even intervene in the physical world? Or are the divine and physical worlds separate universes? Issues such as these, which are of fundamental importance in the book of Job, also play a prominent role in a book that was written in the first half of the twentieth century. It goes without saying, however, that the way in which Tolkien treats such issues differs substantially from the way the author of the book of Job presented them. In this article I shall try to indicate a few elements of the divine and divine interventions in Tolkien's universe. It will become clear that notions like chance and luck are strongly related to the realm of the divine.[4]

I. Tolkien's account of creation

In order to present the divine in Tolkien's universe, I will start with an account that is less known to the general public than *The Lord of the Rings*.[5] This account forms part of a series of tales that are fundamental to the understanding of Tolkien's world.[6] The origins of the tales go back as far as the First World War, and form the basis of the story of the Ring, the earliest stages of which were conceived in 1937.[7] From these descriptions it will become clear that in Tolkien's universe the world of elves and men on the one hand and the world of the divine on the other meet in several ways.

Tolkien's account of his world's theogony and cosmogony is called 'the Music of the Ainur'. Its central notion is that Tolkien's universe is governed by one God. It opens like this: 'There was Eru, the One, who in Arda is called Ilúvatar, and he made first the Ainur, the Holy Ones, that were the offspring of his thought, and they were with him before aught else was made' (*The Silmarillion*, p. 15). The Holy Ones, a kind of angelic or godlike being, are asked by the One to sing before Him on themes He will propound to them. In the end, all together make a Great Music. However, in the harmonious music there also arises discord. The discord is caused by Melkor, one of the Holy Ones, a Lucifer-kind of character, who 'began to conceive thoughts of his own unlike those of his brethren',

> and the melodies which had been heard before foundered in a sea of turbulent sound. But the One sat and hearkened until it seemed that about his throne there was a raging storm, as of dark waters that made war upon another in an endless wrath that would not be assuaged.
> Then the One arose, and the Holy Ones perceived that he smiled; and he lifted up his left hand, and a new theme began amid the storm, like and

yet unlike to the former theme, and it gathered power and had new beauty. But the discord of Melkor rose in uproar and contended with it, and again there was a war of sound more violent than before, until many of the Holy Ones were dismayed and sang no longer, and Melkor had the mastery. Then again the One arose, and the Holy Ones perceived that his countenance was stern; and he lifted up his right hand, and behold! a third theme grew amid the confusion, and it was unlike the others. For it seemed at first soft and sweet, a mere rippling of gentle sound in delicate melodies; but it could not be quenched, and it took to itself power and profundity. And it seemed at last that there were two musics progressing at one time before the seat of the One, and they were utterly at variance. The one was deep and wide and beautiful, but slow and blended with an immeasurable sorrow, from which its beauty chiefly came. The other had now achieved a unity of its own; but it was loud, and vain, and endlessly repeated; and it had little harmony, but rather a clamorous unison as of many trumpets braying upon a few notes. And it essayed to drown the other music by the violence of its voice, but it seemed that its most triumphant notes were taken by the other and woven into its own solemn pattern.

In the midst of this strife, whereat the halls of the One shook and a tremor ran out into the silences yet unmoved, the One arose a third time, and his face was terrible to behold. Then he raised up both his hands, and in one chord, deeper than the Abyss, higher than the Firmament, piercing as the light of the eye of the One, the Music ceased (*The Silmarillion*, pp. 16–17).[8]

This is not a sketch of a contest between symphonies by Anton Bruckner and Glenn Branca, it is Tolkien's view on harmony and discord in Arda, as his world is called. Both harmony and discord find their source in the Holy Ones. These find their origin in the One God. 'Mighty are the Holy Ones, and mightiest among them is Melkor; but that he may know, and all the Holy Ones, that I am the One, those things that ye have sung, I will show them forth, that ye may see what ye have done. And thou, Melkor, shalt see that no theme may be played that hath not its uttermost source in me, nor can any alter the music in my despite. For he that attempteth this shall prove but mine instrument in the devising of things more wonderful, which he himself had not imagined' (*The Silmarillion*, pp. 17–18).

When the One visualizes the Music of the Holy Ones, each of them beholds the different parts of the theme that they had sung. In the visualization by the One things turn out to be fairer and lovelier than they had imagined and conceived. This is even true of the rebellious angel, who will discover that all the secret thoughts of his own mind are but a part of the whole and tributary to its glory. The One then takes away the vision and the Holy Ones perceive darkness, 'which they had not known before except in thought', and this causes unrest among them. After seeing them, the One speaks to them once more: 'I know the desire of your minds that what ye have seen should verily be, not only in your thought, but even as ye yourselves are, and yet other. Therefore I say: *Eä!* Let these things Be! And I will send forth into the Void the Flame Imperishable, and it shall be at the heart of the World, and the World shall Be; and those of you that will may go down into it' (*The Silmarillion*, p. 21).

Some of the Holy Ones stay with the One, and others descend into the world. The world, however, does not at all look like the vision: it is still empty, and void, and darkness lies upon its face, so the Holy Ones have to begin and shape the world during 'ages uncounted and forgotten'. The Holy Ones know the foundations of the earth, they create the stars in the sky, they enter into the springs of the sea and walk in the recesses of the deep. They prepare the world so that it can be inhabited by 'the Children of the One': elves and men – the latter are humankind as we know it from our own every-day world. The elves on the other hand are non-human beings, even though they look human-like. They might be compared to humanity before the fall in Eden: they are immortal, fairer than men, and wise. It is in this world, created by the offspring of the One's thoughts, that the tale of *The Lord of the Rings* is set.[9]

II. Manifestations of the divine in *The Lord of the Rings*

Unlike the creation account given above, the story of the War of the Ring that is recounted in *The Lord of the Rings* does not present many clues about the divine realm or divine beings. That is, unless one is familiar with the accounts from *The Silmarillion*, which the majority of readers are not. Despite the absence of divine beings, there is an unmistakable presence of traces of divine intervention or divine interference throughout *The Lord of the Rings*. This becomes especially clear in those passages in which characters use words that belong to the realm of 'chance, fate and luck'.[10]

A first indication of this can be found in the prologue to *The Lord of the Rings*, in which it is told how the One Ring enters into the ownership of the hobbit Bilbo Baggins.[11] *It was an accident, mere luck*, that Bilbo found the Ring in the dark mines at the roots of the mountains. Bilbo did not have any idea about the Ring's use or where it came from. Nor did he know that it made its wearer invisible. However, when he was being followed by its previous owner, he was saved by his *luck*: 'For as he ran he put his hand in his pocket, and the ring slipped quietly on to his finger' (*The Lord of the Rings*, p. 24).

An important passage in the book is the council during which it is decided that the only way to overthrow the evil power is to destroy the Ring. In the course of the council's discussions, Gandalf the wizard reveals that some years before this meeting he and some others had driven out the evil power from its hiding place. There it had been taking shape and power again: 'and that was in the very year of the finding of this Ring: a strange chance, if chance it was' (*The Lord of the Rings*, 267). Some time before, Gandalf had said to Frodo, who had inherited the Ring, that behind Bilbo's finding of the Ring 'there was something else at work, beyond any design of the Ring-maker. I can put it no plainer than by saying that Bilbo was *meant* to find the Ring, and *not* by its maker. In which case you also were *meant* to have it. And that may be an encouraging thought' (*The Lord of the Rings*, p. 69; italics in the original). A few pages further, this urges Frodo to lament: 'Why did it come to me? Why was I *chosen?*' (*The Lord of the Rings*, p. 74; my italics). Aragorn, a human being who near the end of the book turns out to be the long-awaited King (hence the title of the third volume of the book: *The Return of the King*), shares Gandalf's opinion. During the aforementioned council he says to Frodo: 'it has been ordained that you should hold it for a while.'[12]

Before Frodo and his companions reach one of the last refuges (the place where the council is held), they have met all kinds of misfortune. Having left their village, they are confronted with a Black Rider; they do not have the faintest idea what he might be, or what he might be up to (and he turns out to be a servant of the evil power). The Rider almost captures them, but just before he comes upon them, a group of elves passes by. According to their spokesman, the meeting is 'more than chance', but what its purpose might be, he cannot see (*The Lord of the Rings*, p. 98).

On continuing their journey to this safe harbour, the hobbits end up in 'the Old Forest', where they get into serious trouble. It is very fortunate for them that Tom Bombadil, their saviour, enters the scene. Frodo asks: 'Did you hear me calling, Master, or was it just chance that brought you at that moment?' To which Tom answers that he certainly did not hear him call: 'Just chance brought me then, if chance you call it' (*The Lord of the Rings*, p. 147).

After their three-day sojourn at Bombadil's the hobbits make their acquaintance with Aragorn. He takes them in secrecy to the place where the council is to be held, leading them along paths that are seldom trodden. During this trek he finds a single pale-green jewel: 'It is a beryl, an elf-stone. Whether it was set there, or left by chance, I cannot say; but it brings hope to me' (*The Lord of the Rings*, p. 217). It turns out that it was not chance: one of the elves from the place they are heading for had put it there. There is a similar occurrence later in the book, when two of the hobbits have been kidnapped. One of them can hide himself from their kidnappers' view for a moment, and throws away the brooch of his cloak, hoping that a pursuer may find it. When Aragorn discovers the brooch, he concludes: 'This did not drop by chance; it was cast away as a token to any that might follow' (*The Lord of the Rings*, p. 444).

From these latter passages, one might conclude that 'chance' (or 'luck' or 'fortune'[13]) – isn't that accidental at all. There seems to be a kind of rationale. The same is the case in the words spoken by Gandalf and Aragorn that refer to Frodo's owning of the Ring and which I quoted above. A notion like 'fate', 'that which has been spoken [by the gods]', starts imposing itself upon the reader: 'people have a strong tendency to invent words which express their feeling both that some things are just accidents, and that there may well be some patterning force in just accidents'.[14] In this connection one might also take into consideration the words of the council's chairman about those that participate in the council in which it will be decided how to deal with the Ring. 'That is the purpose for which you are called hither. Called, I say, though I have not called you to me, strangers from distant lands. You have come and are here met, in this very nick of time, by chance as it may seem. Yet it is not so. Believe rather that it is so ordered that we, who sit here, and none others, must now find council for the peril of the world.'[15]

It is by no means impossible that the way 'chance' and 'fortune' are being used in *The Lord of the Rings* indicates the characters' belief of how the divine, or the 'Holy Ones', work in their world. So it is the characters who interpret an event as having happened by 'chance' or 'fortune' – by doing this they introduce forces outside themselves. Several characters in *The Lord of the Rings* appear to consider accidental events providential, which makes them part of a larger design of some higher power. On the other hand, as always it takes two to tango. Apart from the (possible) divine interventions character itself is needed: besides 'fate', 'virtue' is needed too.[16] If providence has 'ordained' that Frodo should bear the Ring, this does not present any implication whatsoever with regard to the way he should act. The characters within the boundaries of the book are all free to act as they like: they do what seems best to them.[17] Boromir, for example, another human being, illustrates that someone need not do the same thing, even though for him there is the same category of 'chance' involved. Destroying the Ring is unthinkable for him, because it might be used to overthrow the Enemy: 'And behold! In our need chance brings to light the Ring of Power. It is a gift, I say; a gift to the foes of Mordor [the land of the evil power]. It is mad not to use it, to use the power of the Enemy against him.' He is not aware of the danger that making use of the Ring will lead to his ruin and to the corruption of his heart and mind. He wants to the take the Ring from Frodo, because 'It is not yours save by unhappy chance. It might have been mine. It should be mine. Give it to me!'[18]

Passages like these present a kind of clue that might give the reader an idea that there is more than meets the eye in Middle-earth. There is also another type of indication that the events in Middle-earth are being strongly influenced by the realm of the divine. This latter type is only touched upon in *The Lord of the Rings*, or rather, it is not prominently present in the book.

A first indication of the existence of such influence from another realm can be derived from Gandalf's words after he has returned from death.[19] He says: 'Naked was I sent back – for a brief time, until my task is done' (*The Lord of the Rings*, p. 524). He gives no information about who sent him back, or even who sent him there before he died! Yet Gandalf's words refer to something beyond the 'ordinary' world. Another character in the book cites something Gandalf once said about the many names born by the wizard. One of these is Olórin. 'Olórin I was in my youth in the West that is forgotten' (*The Lord of the Rings*, p. 697). In the book itself it appears to be clear where this 'West' is to be situated: considering the context in which the phrase occurs, it refers to the western part of Middle-earth. However, the reader who is acquainted with Tolkien's other writings on his invented world (like *The Silmarillion*), knows that the divine realm used to be situated in the West. That reader will also know that Olórin is one of the Holy Ones, who in the beginning shaped the world. The information, provided by both *The Lord of the Rings* and *The Silmarillion*, shows that Gandalf is sent as an emissary to Middle-earth to help elves and men in their struggles against Evil, against the evil power, although this is not stated explicitly in the tale about the War of the Ring.

III. Concluding observations

Tolkien was a Roman Catholic, and that had a profound influence on his work. As he himself wrote in a letter before his epic was published: '*The Lord of the Rings* is of course a fundamentally religious and Catholic work; unconsciously so at first, but consciously in the revision.'[20] Knowing this, it is by no means a surprise that the writings on his world open with an account of creation. In this account it becomes clear that Tolkien's universe is governed by one God. His monotheistic belief resulted in a secondary world that is characterized by monotheism as well. In his universe the One 'creates' the Holy Ones – in contrast to the account in Genesis 1.1–2.4a, the One does not create the world Himself, a task that is accomplished by the Holy Ones. The general fabric of the world, however, comes from the One: He propounds the musical themes on which the Holy Ones make the Great Music. This music is visualized, and in the end materialized as 'the world' by the One. Part of the Holy Ones enter into the world –in which they will remain until the end of time – and help creating it (perhaps these could be compared to the 'angels or messengers of YHWH' in the Bible). In this respect the divine is continuously present in Tolkien's world. To which should be added that the realm in which the Holy Ones dwell is unreachable for men (like the Garden of Eden?). This does not exclude the possibility that from the realm of the Holy Ones emissaries are sent to the world of men, as in the case of Gandalf during the War of the Ring.[21]

A second observation regards the central issue of Tolkien's world. His world is characterized by the ongoing struggle between the forces of evil and, generally speaking, elves and men. This happens throughout his tales. At the same time, as becomes clear again and again, it is obvious that evil cannot be extinguished or banned from the world. As noted before, there is a Lucifer-like being among the Holy Ones. It is he and his followers from whom evil continually arises. Since the Holy Ones find their source in God, evil finds its source in God, in the One, as well. Therefore it will also always be present in the physical world. In Tolkien's view evil is an integral part of existence and cannot be avoided.[22] Yet, in their struggle against evil, elves and men seem to feel supported by the divine. They name certain events 'chance', 'accident', 'luck' or 'fortune', by means of which Providence (or God?) seems to be at work in Middle-earth.

Notes

1. J. R. R. Tolkien, *The Lord of the Rings*, de luxe edition, London: Hyman 1990, p. 913.
2. H. Carpenter, *J. R. R. Tolkien. A Biography*, London: Allen & Unwin 1977, pp. 95–115.
3. Cf. T. Shippey, *J. R. R. Tolkien. Author of the Century*, London: HarperCollins 2000, pp. xx-xxi; see also J. Pearce, *Tolkien: Man and Myth. A Literary Life*, London: HarperCollins 1998, pp. 1–10. In one of the polls *The Lord of the Rings* came only second; the first position was taken by the Bible.
4. This article, in which most space is devoted to *The Lord of the Rings*, gives a brief

introduction to Tolkien's world with regard to its God and its heavenly creatures. This overview does not pretend to be exhaustive.

5. J. R. R. Tolkien, *The Silmarillion* (ed. C. Tolkien), London: George Allen & Unwin 1977. In *The Silmarillion*, published posthumously, Tolkien's son Christopher has tried to present an overview and harmonization of the differing accounts of his father's mythology that were written between 1917 and 1981. The often conflicting versions of Tolkien's mythology have been published in the twelve-volume series *The History of Middle-earth*, ed. C. Tolkien, London 1983–1996.

6. Cf. *The Return of the Shadow* (*The History of Middle-earth*, Vol.VI, ed. C. Tolkien), London: Unwin Hyman 1988.

7. The above quotation is slightly altered: instead of 'the One' the original reads 'Ilúvatar', and instead of 'the Holy Ones' the original reads 'the Ainur'. This happens in all quotations in which the original reads 'the Ainur' and 'Ilúvatar'.

8. Needless to say, *The Lord of the Rings* is only one of many tales that are set in this world.

9. This point is made by T. Shippey, *The Road to Middle-earth*, London: Allen & Unwin 1982, esp. pp. 114–15; cf. P. Meyer Spacks, 'Power and Meaning in *The Lord of the Rings*', in N. D. Isaacs and R. A. Zimbardo, *Tolkien and the Critics. Essays on J. R. R. Tolkien's* The Lord of the Rings, Notre Dame, Indiana: Notre Dame University Press 1968, pp. 81–99. See also G. Urang, *Shadows of Imagination. Religion and Fantasy in the Writings of C. S. Lewis, Charles Williams and J. R. R. Tolkien*, Philadelphia: Pilgrim Press 1971, pp. 113–20.

10. Hobbits are a species invented by Tolkien. In the Prologue to *The Lord of the Rings*, he says: 'Hobbits are an unobtrusive but very ancient people ... Their height is variable, ranging between two and four feet of our measure' (pp. 14–15). From the prologue it becomes clear that they are in one way or another related to humanity. They very much resemble Victorian Englishmen in a kind of pre-modern society.

11. *The Lord of the Rings*, p. 264. Aragorn has several Christ-like features – just like the book, he is strongly influenced by Tolkien's Catholicism; cf. my 'God in Middle-earth?', in B. Verstappen et al. (eds), *Vreemde verhalen, goed nieuws? Over Harry Potter en andere helden*, Nijmegen: Valkhof Pers 2003, pp. 94–111; also see my 'Tom Bombadil's Biblical Connections', *Mallorn. The Journal of the Tolkien Society* 37, 1999, pp. 15–18.

12. 'Fortune or fate helped you', Gandalf concludes, when Frodo was not stabbed in the heart, but only suffered a wound in his shoulder from the attack by Black Riders.

13. Shippey, *Author of the Century* (n.3), p. 145.

14. *The Lord of the Rings*, p. 259. Cf. the words of Galadriel, the Elven queen: 'Maybe the paths that you each shall tread are already laid before your feet, though you do not see them' (*The Lord of the Rings*, p. 388).

15. 'Besides, one must grasp one's faith, otherwise it is possible that it will not come

about: fate needs virtue' (O. Marquard, 'Ende des Schicksals? Einige Bemerkungen über die Unvermeidlichkeit des Unverfügbaren', in O. Marquard et al., *Schicksal? Grenzen der Machbarkeit. Ein Symposion*, Munich: Deutscher Taschenbuch Verlag 1977, pp. 7–26: 8.

16. Cf. Gandalf: 'All we have to decide is what to do with the time that is given us' (*The Lord of the Rings*, p. 64).

18. *The Lord of the Rings*, pp. 418–19.

19. For clarity's sake and because of lack of space, I will not deal with the references to Elbereth (as in the hymn '*A Elbereth Gilthoniel*'), or with the three occasions on which the Valar, who are part of the Holy Ones, are mentioned (*The Lord of the Rings*, pp. 687, 871 and 1004).

20. H. Carpenter (ed.), *The Letters of J. R. R. Tolkien*, London: Allen & Unwin, 1981, p. 172. The letter is dated 2 December 1953.

21. Tolkien called Gandalf an *angelos* in one of his letters (H. Carpenter, ed., *The Letters of J. R. R. Tolkien*, p. 202).

22. An interesting discussion of Tolkien's concept of evil can be found in Shippey, *Author of the Century* (n.3), pp. 130–42.

From Father to the Needy to Brother of Jackals and Companion of Ostriches: A Meditation on Job

ELSA TAMEZ

For Latin Americans the book of Job is a paradigm of protest by those who suffer unjustly. It is also a biblical source that provides a different way of speaking of the God of grace, from 'among the ashes' (NRSV).[1] Job's cries of demand for justice are so powerful that those who suffer unjustly focus all their attention on Job's disgraced and abandoned life. Little attention is paid to his previous life – a rich and revered man, pious and compassionate to the poor. Little account is taken of the 'happy ending', and none of Job's wounding strictures on the 'senseless, disreputable brood . . . whipped out of the land' (cf. 30.1–10). In other words, the power of the Latin American reading has almost always been in its identification and solidarity with two voices expressing suffering through unjust poverty, disease and abandonment: Job's cries and those of the excluded of today.

These voices, however, sometimes conjoin and sometimes separate. If Job has served as a mirror held up to the current reality of injustice, Job has also had to learn from the Latin American people's long experience of injustice. Portions of the following 'Letter to Job'[2] reflect this situation of intertwining of the voices and their distancing. This letter was written at the beginning of the 1980s, the period of the most sinister dictatorships in Central America. In this meditation I propose to analyse the harmony of the voices and their differentiation on the basis of this letter and of new elements in the current situation.

Job is addressed as brother. He is no longer the 'father to the needy' (29.16) he once was, to whom all, rich and poor, paid homage when he came among them (29.1–11); he is the Job who is 'a brother of jackals, and a companion of ostriches' (30.29).

Brother Job,
Your cries of pain and protest have struck into our bones, have deprived

us of sleep; blood flows from our ears. Your hands move in all directions: they point to us, strike us, implore us, they court us, caress us, push us – where are you taking us, friend Job? Your stench of death has invaded our noses; we smell you everywhere. Your skeletal body goads us. Pieces of your rotted flesh hang from our flesh: you have infected us, brother Job; you have infected us, our families, our people. And your look of longing for justice and your breath full of fury have filled us with courage, tenderness, and hope.

When the pious-wealthy Job ceases to be so and falls into misfortune, he joins the world of the wretched. His horrifying shouts of pain and his protests against injustice make it possible for those who suffer an equal fate to lose their timidity. Identification and solidarity come into being. Job's stage becomes a mirror. Through his life, staged as a tragedy, we look at our own situation and are challenged. Because the life of the world of the wretched that we know did not come into being overnight, as happened to Job. It has been developing over five hundred years, and because we are so used to living it in this way we risk believing it to be natural and simply the will of God. With his protests, Job helps to change those who have forgotten that life was not given for it to be lived in misery. Job calls us to protest against the suffering of the innocent. And so:

> How brave you are, brother! What powers of endurance you have! You are a spectre, as we are, ill, abandoned, despised, oppressed. You make us sick (Do we make people sick?). Your friends Eliphaz, Bildad and Zophar go on torturing you and giving you bad counsel. They tell you it is a sin to protest and to uphold your innocence, that God has punished you, and that you need to repent. And you, friend, despite everything, don't give in; you cry out the louder. You don't believe them and you struggle against them. What's more, you dare to rail against God Almighty: you accuse him of causing your misfortunes, of staying silent in the face of your suffering. You contend with him, with the one who was your friend and who has abandoned you and you don't know why. You proclaim that you have been just and innocent. You have every right to defend yourself because you are human. It is every man and woman's right to raise their voice against unjust suffering.

In Latin America Job is admired for his endurance, for his courage in not accepting things as they are. The Job-mirror makes us see our own reality more crudely; it is a spectre that makes us sick. But since he is 'like us', a painful question, submerged in the discourse, slowly emerges: 'Do we make people sick ourselves?' It is a thought that comes to mind only when we know what it is to make people sick through someone who makes them sick. What is admirable is that the one who is making them sick does not hold out his hand snivelling and asking for justice like a beggar with lowered eyes and his tail between his legs. He protests against those who face him: the counsellors, God, and even the young 'whose fathers I would have disdained to set with the dogs of my flock' (30.1). He protests against his friends because their theology is no use, against God because he does not appear to support him, and against the disreputable because they mock him. Job's protests reaffirm the right of the Latin American people to protest against injustice. First against conquest, then against dictatorship, and now against economic globalization.

Faced with the dilemma which the book poses and which corrals Job into seeing God from a very narrow viewpoint ('If Job is innocent, God is guilty; if God is just, Job deserves his punishment'), in Latin America the character of Job is invited to walk other paths, since long experience of injustice has made our people expert in looking for ways out. Job has not had this experience. However righteously he may have treated the poor and widows and orphans, he was very far from knowing the world of the wretched. It is very difficult for him to see alternatives when he knows only one way of experiencing God, through a comfortable relationship based on well-being and on a narrow theology marked by the doctrine of retribution. His experience among the ashes makes him protest, but as his experience of living like this is sudden and fortuitous, he is incapable of discerning a new way of knowing God and speaking of God. Our people, who have listened to God among the ashes of several centuries, can counsel him. From here, we can challenge Job too:

> But let us also keep silent, comrade Job. Let us not complain any more. We have made enough lamentation. Your wise speech closed the mouths of the wise men. They no longer have any arguments or any god to back them up. Let us close our mouths and listen. Let us allow God to appear before us and give an account of his silences. God's silences are mysterious, sometimes filling us with terror, paralysing us in the face of the legion of demons who crush the life out of human beings. But without these mysterious silences of God we cannot be human. When God speaks a lot, human beings fall silent. They fail to hear the shouts of the poor, of those who suffer. They become dumb beasts, do not journey, do not wait, can do nothing, bear nothing. God is silent so that human beings may speak,

protest, struggle. God keeps quiet because he wants human beings to be human. When God remains silent and human beings weep, God weeps in solidarity with them, but he does not intervene; he waits for their cry of protest.

Our people know how to listen to God, how to feel God. If they could not listen to and feel God, the cultures of our forbears would by now have disappeared; we would have been extinguished for lack of faith and inability to withstand so much injustice and so many lies. We hope in God in some form, without ever knowing how God will respond, but in the certainty that he will respond. Sometimes – often – for some people it feels as though God has gone away on a very long journey and disappeared for good, but ultimately we know that God is there, always present, or that he will come back. We usually see God in small things, but then they never seem small: a neighbour's act of solidarity or the fruit of prickly pears. 'Curse God and die' (2.9) also forms part of those voices that rise up from among our people out of the depths of their justified discontent, when they reach the limits of God's silence. But they do not consider them 'foolish', as Job does (2.10). They are rebel voices, ultimately asking for the tenderness of solidarity besides justice; those who say they hate God are in reality weeping at his absence, and so their curses call forth not rejection but the embraces of those sensitive to the great need to satisfy the body, the great need to have God present. Job needed that attitude from his friends Eliphaz, Bildad and Zophar, not their rejection for referring to God as an adversary and accusing him of injustice. The counsels in the letter to Job are attempts at replying to ourselves. They help in some way to justify – to ourselves – God's absence, but above all they help us to bear it.

The new language about God, apart from that in Job's protest, appears in the two speeches by God, when God dialogues with Job and challenges him.

Then God speaks once more, but in dialogue with us. He shows us how mountain goats and deer push their young away, so that they become strong, grow up in the open, and do not come back for milk (cf. 39.4). God shows us how the wild ass is free, 'scorns the tumult of the city . . . does not hear the shouts of the driver [and] ranges the mountains for its pasture' (39.7–8). The wild ox refuses to spend nights in its stable; ostriches 'laugh at the horse and its rider' (39.18); horses snort majestically, go out to meet weapons and have no fear (39.20–22); eagles nest in the highest places, from where they spy out their faraway prey (39.26–30). God gives all of these that strength and that freedom. So let's get up, brother Job, since you can't catch Leviathan with a fishhook or the monster Behemoth with a snare. They are powerful forces that only God's strength in our strength can overcome. The Lord challenges us: let us meet his challenge.

Such language, which Gustavo Gutiérrez calls the language of contemplation, is quite familiar to our people. One has to remember that prophetic discourse is not the language of everyone but of those with a raised political awareness, who can help to arouse awareness in their brothers and sisters. The language of our humble people, based on nature more than anything and on observation of everyday things, is filled with wisdom through contemplation. This makes them more able than Job to listen to the voice of God and to dialogue through his creation and through gestures among themselves. Job is unable to do so: God has to intervene directly and teach him to be adult, to be independent, so that he may stop complaining. His past life does not let him do so: a wealthy city-dweller, conditioned by codes of honour, with a privileged position in the city, without worries over his daily bread, tied to God's apron strings like a pet, seeking to be rewarded for something that is his duty as a human being: acting justly and supportively toward the poor and defenceless. The letter from the people of Latin America teaches Job how to set about overcoming his deplorable state, freeing himself from the last dregs of his mercantilist dependence on God, marked out by exchange of goods – things traded for worship. Wild animals are strong and free: God takes care of their freedom. God is free, Job is free; peoples should not be domesticated by mercantilist relationships either with God or among their fellow human beings.

Job, now called 'brother Job', has to raise himself up from the ashes and stop struggling with the Almighty, since he has little to gain from it. The experience of our peoples makes them know this better than Job. They understand that it is important for him to protest and admire his bravery, but for our people challenging God goes beyond identifying the guilty parties. The power of evil defies us all, including Almighty God: Leviathan, as God says, has no equal on earth (41.33). Job has to pull himself up to re-order God's creation, to become God's helpmate and companion, but without killing all the wicked whom he encounters on his way in order to make God's justice shine (40.11–14), since God's mercy is as great as Behemoth and Leviathan. Those who suffer unjustly do not seek the end of the perverse but that of perversion, even if at times they utter imprecatory prayers for their annihilation in order to relieve their pain a little. If they believe that 'another world is possible', it is because they know that ultimately both Behemoth and Leviathan are creatures like human beings, and

Behemoth 'eats grass like an ox' (40.15); they can be tamed, and God, one way or another, has them under control.

Job's experience of suffering enabled him to some extent to enter into the world of the wretched and so get to know other people's suffering. This experience inevitably led him to change his outlook. His reinstatement at the end of the book confronts him with dichotomies that do not surface in the book but that the poor-abandoned-sick, not reinstated, are still posing today.

> Now, friend Job, you have really known God. You will never be the same after this experience of pain. You will never go back to being that rich man to whom everything was handed on a plate, who gave to have-nots out of what he had left over. You have known the essence of the wretched, and no one will be able to erase that experience from your story. Now you know God better. God reinstated you because you struggled against him and with him until he blessed you. What will you do now? God reinstated you – and us? We await you down among the ashes.

As we see it, Job's experience among the ashes enabled him to know God better – the side of God that he did not know when he had everything. Job crossed, without wanting to, the divide that separates a sunlit and abundant world from a dark world, unknown and fearful for those who live on the light side. Two different experiences of God in the light of different realities: it is not the same to be father and protector of the poor as to be 'a brother of jackals and a companion of ostriches'. On the light side there is security, show, and homage (29); on the dark side there is insecurity, abandonment, and struggle to survive (30). This, however, is what is seen from afar, particularly from the far side, the light one. When you live among the poor and wretched, the invisibility of light in the darkness, caused above all by the strength of the light on the other side, disappears as your eyes become accustomed to this world. As you learn to live together, a light gradually penetrates the darkness, enabling you to see the faces and lives of the wretched in a different way: they are less monstrous than you imagined them to be from the distance of the other side; they are faces and lives lived in a much more human, free, and supportive way – human vices, such as rivalry and violence, are always present, it's true, but no more than in the light world, where appearance and lies dominate more. The experience of God is different in each world.

Latin Americans, poor and believing, feel solidarity with Job, but they switch off when Job nostalgically recounts his previous life of such great abundance, which was so pleasant for him but shows up the contrasts of a divided and discriminatory society. They look the other way when Job in his suffering longs for the homage paid to him when he went into the city square and took his place in the assembly. There, Job recalls, 'the young men saw me and withdrew, and the aged rose up and stood; the nobles refrained from talking, and laid their hands on their mouths . . . They listened to me, and waited, and kept silence for my counsel' (see 29.7–25). These nostalgic reminiscences of Job, including that of being 'a father to the needy', cannot fail to remind us of the tributes paid today to landowner bosses.

For our people, the words Job uses to contrast his past life with his present wretched state are more painful:

> But now they make sport of me,
>   those who are younger than I,
> whose fathers I would have disdained
>   to set with the dogs of my flock.
> What could I gain from the strength of their hands?
>   All their vigour is gone.
> Through want and hard hunger
>   they gnaw the dry and desolate ground,
> they pick mallow and the leaves of bushes,
>   and to warm themselves the roots of broom.
> They are driven out from society;
>   people shout after them as after a thief.
> In the gullies of wadis they must live,
>   in holes in the ground, and in the rocks.
> Among the bushes they bray;
>   under the nettles they huddle together.
> A senseless, disreputable brood,
>   they have been whipped out of the land (30.1–8).

It hurts to hear these verses from Job's mouth: they are shunned out of solidarity with his suffering and his claim for justice. But we read them out of the corner of our eyes and feel their words hitting us like stones: a betrayal for some, or lack of understanding on Job's part for others. These wounding sentiments from Job show that he has only half crossed the threshold, in his body but not in his mind and his outlook. Perhaps this is why the inhabitants of this world, the one seen as dark, make fun of him – because laughing at him is like laughing at the decadence of a world of light far from the wretched. In these texts we part company with Job, since we are looking for real brotherhood, not just with the poor who hope in God but with the ragged and the rootless, with the jackals and the ostriches. Let Job take his own words seriously and live up to them, when he says that he is a brother of jackals and companion of ostriches.

Job uses the language of the world on 'the other side' to refer to the wretched who live on 'this side', because he perhaps never really got to know this world properly. The Salvadoran poet Roque Dalton, through his 'Poem of love',³ can teach Job that its inhabitants are also his brothers and compatriots:

> Those who widened the Panama Canal,
> those who repaired the Pacific fleet
> in the bases of California,
> those who rotted in the prisons of Guatemala,
> Mexico, Honduras, Nicaragua,
> for being robbers, smugglers, swindlers,
> for being hungry,
> the usual suspects for everything,
> the girls who filled the bars and brothels
> in every port and capital of the region,
> those who sow maize in foreign jungles,
> the kings of the night courts,
> those whose origin no one ever knows,
> the best craftsmen in the world,
> those who were peppered with shot as they crossed the border,
> those who died of malaria
> or scorpion bites or yellow fever
> in the hell of banana plantations,
> those who wept drunkenly at the national anthem
> under a pacific cyclone or northern snows,
> the parasites, the beggars, the stoned,
> the simple-minded sons of the great whore,
> those who only just managed to get back,
> those who were a little luckier,
> the eternally undocumented,
> the do-alls, sell-alls, eat-alls,
> the first to draw a knife,
> the saddest of the world's sad,
> *my compatriots,*
> *my brothers.*

The letter to Job ends with the ever-present question: When will the situation change between us on this earth? Job's compatriots and brothers are still waiting for him among the ashes.

Translated by Paul Burns

Notes

1. Gustavo Gutiérrez sees the book of Job as made up of both prophetic discourse and contemplation, with the latter indispensable for an understanding that moves beyond the received wisdom and is open to the unexpected. See his *On Job: God-Talk and the Suffering of the Innocent*, Maryknoll, NY 1987.
2. Elsa Tamez, 'Carta a Job', *Páginas* 53.2, 1983, p. 39. Some paragraphs of the letter have been omitted here.
3. Some parts of the poem have been omitted for the sake of clarity. The italics are mine.

Reading Job 'Positively' in the Context of HIV/AIDS in South Africa

GERALD WEST with BONGI ZENGELE

Introduction

As I will be writing here about reading the Bible with people who are living with HIV and AIDS I begin with some words of caution. I worry when well-intentioned people who are not HIV-positive prescribe what kind of biblical texts are relevant for people who are. The question of what and how we read the Bible in the context of HIV/AIDS must be substantially constituted by actual collaboration with people who are living with the virus. We are all affected, and we are all being partially constituted by the daily realities of HIV/AIDS, but we are not all infected. Alongside the other liberation theologies that have shaped our African contexts – and I speak here speci-fically of liberation theologies that have centred upon race, class, gender and culture – HIV/AIDS must now take its place.[1] And what an HIV/AIDS liberation theology demands is that we grant an epistemological privilege to the *experience* of those who are infected. Per Frostin is correct when he says that the distinguishing characteristic of liberation theologies is not content but methodology,[2] and the key to the methodology of liberation theologies is the epistemological privileging of those who experience that particular marginalization. Those who know the lived reality of HIV/AIDS must become the primary interlocutors of theology.[3]

A personal story here will highlight this important point. At a tea-time discussion in the School of Theology at the University of KwaZulu-Natal, where I teach, our conversation turned to the subject of Jesus' humanity and divinity (tea-times in our school do sometimes generate serious theological discussion!). In this relaxed and somewhat experimental context I ventured to suggest that just as Jesus was claimed to be black by African American black theology and was claimed to be female by feminist theology, so a theo-logy of HIV/AIDS might claim the blood of Jesus to be HIV-positive. It seemed to me that such a claim would be in continuity with the similar theo-logical claims of kindred struggles. A colleague, Phumzile Zondi-Mabizela, who is HIV-positive, responded by saying that she felt uncomfortable with this, and she then went on to say how important theologically it was to her to see the blood of Jesus as not HIV-positive. She found hope in his HIV-negative blood.[4]

My second introductory point is related to this first comment. In the South African context lived realities are not unifocal; they are not about one 'issue'. Marginalization in South Africa is historically intersected. Race, class, gender and culture are all factors in the epidemiology of the disease in our country. The hard work and careful analysis that has begun to generate a more contextually relevant theology must be sustained while we mainstream this 'new' thread, as we facilitate a mutually transformative dialogue among the epistemological realities of marginalization in our context.

My third and final introductory comment is that any attempt to talk theology without at the same time being engaged in practical action for appropriate and holistic health care (in the full sense of the word) for those infected is obscene. Part of our task is to ensure suitable treatment for all[5] and part of our task is to tackle stigma and discrimination. This article takes up the latter task.

I. The texts positive people prefer

Taking my opening point seriously, I must confess that our experience in the Institute of the Study of the Bible and Worker Ministry Project (ISB&WM) – a project which operates in the interface between socially engaged biblical scholars and ordinary poor, working-class and marginalized readers of the Bible – in working with those who have tested positive for HIV and who have joined our Siyaphila support group for people living with HIV/AIDS is that they seem to prefer New Testament texts to Old Testament texts.[6] Having said this, however, I should perhaps be more precise. The Bible studies facilitated by Bongi Zengele, our Coordinator of the Solidarity Programme for People Living with HIV/AIDS, and one of the founders of the Siyaphila support groups, clearly show a preference for texts in which Jesus stands with those whom society has marginalized. So it is not necessarily the New Testament as a whole that is found to be affirming of their human dignity, but particular texts within the New Testament. As research into the reading patterns of Africans indicates, African Christians may actually prefer the Old Testament.[7] Again, this is perhaps not nuanced enough, for it is not the Old Testament as the Old Testament that is at issue, just as it is not the New Testament as the New Testament that is the issue for members of the Siyaphila support group. What is at issue are the lines of connection or resonance between the lived faith of African Christians and particular biblical texts. So, because much of the Old Testament resonates with the socio-religious realities of African Christians,[8] it is the Old Testament that forms the bulk of their favourite biblical passages. Interestingly, in the context of HIV/AIDS, it is the New Testament that is providing sites of connection with the lived realities of ordinary African Christians who are living with HIV/AIDS. They are drawn to a Jesus who continually identifies with those whom society has marginalized. What, then, does the book of Job contribute? I begin with another word of caution.

II. Dominant theologies in the Old Testament

Job, and the Old Testament generally, presents a problem to those living with HIV/AIDS, because it appears to have such a clear dominant theology.[9] This predominant theology is known as the theology of retribution, and closely related to it is its corollary theology, a theology that emphasizes a God who is totally in control. Briefly, the theology of retribution argues that what people sow, they will reap. As the saying suggests, the metaphor for this form of theology comes from agriculture, and the saying (like the theology) probably has its origins in the early agricultural experience of ancient 'Israel'.[10] In a context in which each family had its tribal land, experience would generally show that those who worked diligently and hard would reap plentiful crops, while those who were lazy and neglectful of their land would suffer hardships. This reality of agricultural life was generalized into other aspects of community life. Given that God was in control of all spheres of life, the argument would go, and not just agriculture, those who lived good lives would reap goodness and those who lived bad lives would reap badness.

However, as Gunther Wittenberg has carefully argued,[11] this community wisdom became distorted as the context changed. With the rise of the monarchy and centralized state, new pressures were brought to bear on the relatively settled and stable agricultural life of ordinary 'Israelites'. Before the monarchy, communities would have had to deal with some unpredictable external factors, such as drought, locusts, and invasions from neighbouring peoples (eg. the Philistines). While the monarchy brought with it security against invasions by providing a standing army, the king, his court and the army all had to eat, and they were not producers. So, as Samuel warns the people in 1 Samuel 8 when they come to him to ask for a king to govern them 'like other nations', the centralized monarchic state must extract food and labour in the form of tribute and taxes from those living on the land. Now it is no longer true that what you sow you reap! You sow, but others in addition to you and your family take and consume what you have produced. In other words, the experience of ordinary people living on the land is no longer the same as it was; it is now possible to work diligently and hard and still not to live well because your resources are being taken by the centralized monarchic state to sustain itself.

However, as Wittenberg shows, this change in experience did not lead to a change in theology, at least not initially. As we know, theological systems are slow to change! What happened, according to Wittenberg, is that the theology remained but became inverted. Before, when people worked diligently it was generally accepted that they would reap the benefits of conforming to God's order. In order to sustain this theology of retribution under the new centralized monarchic system a shift in perspective was required. Now those who showed signs of prosperity were assumed to have done what is right before God. Now, it was argued, what you reaped indicated what you must have sown!

The problem with this theology, of course, is that those who prospered by unjust means were presumed to have lived justly. Many houses and full barns, fine clothes and livestock, and extravagant imported goods were seen by society as signs of God's blessing for a good life. Remarkably, even though there was clear evidence to the contrary, this distorted theology of retribution endured. God, it was assumed, was in control, and so those who prospered must have pleased God by living according to God's order.

This kind of theology has little understanding of structural injustice, and those who have advocated it tend to be those who benefit from systemic privilege, be it the racial privilege of apartheid, the middle-class privilege of capitalism, or the male privilege of patriarchy. What we now need to recognize is the devastating effects of this theology on people living with HIV/AIDS.

III. AIDS as a punishment from God

Given my analysis, it is not surprising that the predominant view in most Christian communities is that HIV/AIDS is a punishment from God. That HIV is transmitted mainly by sexual intercourse (in our context) only confirms this opinion. Further corroboration of this position is found, according to Habbakuki Lwendo, from aspects of African religion.[12] There is no doubt that this is the dominant theology that people living with HIV/AIDS encounter in our South African society, both in and outside the church. They bear in their bodies God's punishment for their 'sins', particularly their sexual 'sins.'

Fortunately, trajectories[13] or parts of the Old Testament interrupt this theology. The book of Job is an excellent example.[14] In the prose prologue we enter a world in which the theology of retribution is taken seriously. Job, we are told, was not only himself 'blameless and upright, one who feared God and turned away from evil' (1.1), but he would also 'send and sanctify' his sons and daughters after they had feasted, rising 'early in the morning and offering burnt offerings according to the number of them all; for Job said, "It may be that my children have sinned, and cursed God in their hearts"' (1.5, NRSV). Job's health and wealth, and the health and wealth of his sons and daughters, it is implied, are directly related to Job's righteous life. The theology of retribution holds.

The story then becomes complicated, particularly for the reader, who is privy to the heavenly debate between God and his colleague, the Satan (1.6–12). Job, however, is unaware of the heavenly wager (though its victim), and so is forced to live in a world which, from his perspective, no longer conforms to the principle of retribution. Job has lived righteously – all agree – but is punished rather than rewarded. At first Job doggedly accepts his fate, refusing to question God's control. So much so that he can say, having experienced the loss of his livestock and servants, the destruction of his property and the death of all of his children, and his own deteriorating health, 'the Lord gave, and the Lord has taken away; blessed be the name of the Lord' (1.21). Even the theologically astute call of his wife to put an end to his suffering by questioning God's so-called, alleged, order – Do you still persist in your integrity (i.e. your theology)? Curse God, and die' (2.9) – is met with an affirmation of God's control from her husband: 'Shall we receive the good at the hand of God, and not receive the bad?' (2.10).

Job, it would appear, accepts 'the bad' from God, remaining silent, refusing to 'sin with his lips' (2.10) by questioning God or this theology. As he sits silently his friends come among him, to 'console and comfort him' (2.11). And we know what they will say; they will each explain to him how he must have sinned, in some sense, for how else can he (or, more importantly, they) explain his suffering. By looking at the destroyed and diseased Job they can tell that God must be punishing him in some way for something he has done – this is how their theology works.

But before they can say anything, and to their credit they do not immediately 'counsel' Job, Job speaks. At last he takes his wife's advice! Perhaps the death and destruction around him and within him had numbed him; one hopes so. Now, however, the radical challenge of his wife has registered in his numbed mind; the marvellous ambiguity of the Masoretic text's 'Bless/curse God, and die' have their theological effect. If being righteous and blessing God brings about such havoc, then what damage can cursing God do? Having earlier refused to 'sin with his lips' he now lets rip! Perhaps reluctant to follow his wife's theological proposition the whole way, Job curses God indirectly rather than directly, cursing 'the day of his birth' (3.1). Prose is no longer adequate for what Job is about to say, and so the text shifts into poetry. This shift is more than a shift from prose to poetry, however, it is also a shift in theology!

Here are the beginnings of another theology; here is a cry of rage and pain; here is an incipient and inchoate theology. Here is an attempt to undo what God did in Genesis 1! God says, 'Let there be light' (Genesis 1:3); Job counters with, 'Let the day be darkness!'.[15] Here Job struggles with how to speak of God – how to do theology – in the context of immense suffering and loss. Would that we read this text at the countless funerals of our people who have died from AIDS-related illnesses. Would that Job 3:3–26 were read rather than Job 1.21, 'the Lord gave, and the Lord has taken away; blessed be the name of the Lord'.

Funerals do dominate the daily realities of people in South Africa. Traditionally held on Saturdays, they are also encroaching on Sundays and even weekdays, such is the devastation of the AIDS pandemic.[16] And even though most of the young people in the Siyaphila groups do not attend church on a regular basis, either having been driven out of the church by a perverted theology of HIV/AIDS or having left the church for some other reason, they do encounter the church at funerals. Funerals are a very important part of their lives, as they are for most members of the black African community from which all the group members come. Unfortunately, however, because most of the funerals they attend are for young people like themselves, young people who are estranged from the church, the minister who conducts the funeral often has to be hired by the family for the funeral. The minister of the church which the family attends will often not conduct the funeral of a young person who is suspected of dying of HIV/AIDS related illnesses who has not been a regular member of the church. The hired minister therefore does not have specific ties to the deceased and so feels free to use the opportunity to preach and rail against the evils of HIV/AIDS (and those living with HIV/AIDS), though this is usually done euphemistically and by innuendo, it being culturally and theologically taboo to talk about such things publically.[17]

Attending so many funerals, members of the Siyaphila groups do encounter the book of Job, but usually only the oft-quoted verses in Job 1.21, 'the Lord gave, and the Lord has taken away; blessed be the name of the Lord'. Again, for those infected here is further confirmation that AIDS is a punishment from God. Unfortunately, Job 3 is not read at funerals. But what if it were?

IV. Reading Job 3 'positively'

I took this question to a local Pietermaritzburg Siyaphila group on 11 March. Having raised the question with Bongi Zengele, she invited me to co-facilitate a Bible study with this Siyaphila group. I asked her if she would read Job 3 in isiZulu, but before she did this I introduced the Bible study to Ntombenhle Ngcobo, Thembi Ndawo, Nonhlanhla Zuma, Mduduzi Mshengu, Hlengiwe Zulu, Nelly Nene, S'fiso Zuma, Fikile Ngcobo, Jabu Molefe, Xolani Khumalo, S'bongile Shezi and Phindile Ndlovu.[18]

I asked the group if they knew of the book of Job, and many said they did. I then asked if they had heard Job read in church and funerals, and most said that they knew Job 1.21, 'the Lord gave, and the Lord has taken away; blessed be the name of the Lord'. I followed this up by briefly sketching the literary context of this text, before asking Zengele to read Job chapter 3. Fortunately, as I had been a little late to arrive, the group had already had the opportunity to read the text for themselves.

After Zengele had read Job 3, we[19] asked the group to say what they thought about this text. The first response came from a young man who asked me what could have happened to Job to make him curse the day of his birth. I was impressed that he had grasped the thrust of the poetry so easily and was tempted not to answer him directly, but merely to acknowledge his response and then wait for others to share their thoughts. But I quickly saw that the others were waiting for my response. This had been a genuine, not a rhetorical, question. I responded by going over chapters 1 and 2 in more detail, cataloguing the calamities that had come upon Job's homestead. He nodded at this, but did not say anything more at this point.

The next person to respond was a young woman who drew our attention to verse 18, commenting that she and those who had been diagnosed as HIV-positive felt just like prisoners. This was followed by another member of the group asking, with great yearning, why things like this happened/happen. My response was: 'This is precisely Job's question!' At this point the young man who had set the discussion in motion re-entered, saying that the heading to this section in the isiZulu Bible, 'Job curses the day of his birth', was most apt. This is exactly how he felt on the day he was diagnosed. He literally cursed the day he had been born.

Another member, someone who had not yet spoken, joined the discussion by saying that she thought this text showed that the more faith you had the more you would be tested. My first impulse was to question this, and I did, by wondering aloud whether Job himself would have agreed with her. However, even as I said this it struck me that she was perhaps making a positive comment about herself, namely, that because of her great faith she was now being greatly tested.

The discussion then turned again to Job's cursing his birth, but this time it was followed up by a number of members agreeing that they too had seriously considered taking their own lives. Again they asked me quite directly what advice I had for them concerning this. Given their situation, what about the option of them taking their lives? As one person said, 'We are like Job; we are good people who were not looking for this thing, and yet now we are infected.' So close was their identification with Job and his deep depression. At this moment I realized the dangers of the Bible study and began to wonder if this was not just another misguided attempt to offer resources by a non-infected person. I looked at Bongi Zengele, desperately searching for some signal from her, for some reassurance that I was not leading this group down a road of self-destruction. I worried that I was undoing the many careful months of Siyaphila's self-building work. Her smile reassured me, so I plunged on, saying that I did not think that Job was contemplating taking his own life. For him, I suggested, it was God who was responsible for his life, and until God took it, he was not going to keep silent and accept the dominant theology of his day. He was going to take his considerable anger directly to God and call God to account.

I then quickly voiced my fear by asking the group directly whether this text was of any help to them or was it just a reminder of their desperation. The response was unanimous, but varied. They found the text immensely empowering. So I asked them in what ways they found it empowering. One of the group linked her experience directly to my comments, saying that she found the text comforting, because like Job, the day she received her HIV results she wondered why God had not taken her life earlier, when as a child she had almost drowned. Others said that chapter 3 affirmed the enormous anger they had and that it was theologically permissible to express this anger. Bongi Zengele confirmed this, reminding the group of all they had been through together, specifically of how important it had been for them to learn that it was 'okay' to own all their feelings, even if this required cursing God in prayer. The group agreed, with someone adding that this kind of emotional freedom also contributed to their dealing with other matters unrelated to HIV and AIDS. By expressing their anger, Zengele continued, they had begun to find healing, for both their psyches and their bodies.

The terrible thing, they agreed, was that the church silenced their anger. And so I was challenged directly, with one of the members asking whether I would be willing to lead this kind of Bible study with a wider grouping, including their families and churches. Others assented, making it clear that they felt that this kind of Bible study on this kind of text would make a huge difference to prevailing views. They acknowledged that many people they knew simply had no opportunity to share about these things.

A young man who had said very little in the discussion thus far interrupted this flow by asking me, 'What about those who do deserve it?' By now I was used to this kind of direct request. Again, I drew them back to the text by saying that I thought that Job was having to rethink thoroughly the very notion that people 'deserved' suffering. I went on, and here I was drawing on Elsa Tamez's 'A letter to Job', [20] saying that Job's suffering had taken him out of his comfortable life-style and had shown him the suffering of others.

A young woman then brought the discussion back to where we had started, narrating how she had begun the process of killing herself, using alcohol, until she had realized that she still had responsibilities to her dependdnts. She understood this realization as God calling her back to life, even though she had cursed God. This echoed what had been said earlier, that they were amazed to discover from Job that even though they cursed God, God still welcomed them. I had mentioned in my introductory comments that despite Job's unrelenting outbursts against his friends, the theology they represented and God, God had affirmed that Job 'had spoken of me what is right' (Job 42.7). I re-read this final God speech and wondered aloud whether, by engaging so fully with God, Job had come see God more fully.

These comments of mine, and the explicit comparison of Job and his friends in these verses, prompted a number of the group to talk about their experiences of being judged by their families and friends and churches. One young woman said people in her church had judged her, unjustly, once they knew she was HIV-positive. This text, she said, was a 'homecoming'. A young man then shared how he had been talked about in his community when he had begun to lose weight. It had been very hard, he said, to be the object of other people's judgmental attitudes. However, he had learned to cope with this, he said, through the resources of the Siyaphila group, including this Bible study. What he had learned from the group and this Bible study was that even people close to God face difficulties. Finally, another young man, the same one who had asked about those who might 'deserve it',

commented on how he and other activists were judged when they did awareness work in their communities. People asked them, assuming they were
HIV-positive, 'Now where is your God?' He now knew how to respond, he
shared with us, by saying, 'Job shows that God stays with him.'

At this point there was a pause in the discussion. The group seemed
satisfied with what had been said. Bongi Zengele allowed the quiet to persist,
nodding encouragingly at each member, affirming their openness and their
contributions. She then brought this part of our Bible study to an end by
saying that though their bodies were HIV-positive, they were more than
their bodies. They were spiritual beings as well. Siyaphila, she went on to
say, deliberately worked for an integration of the spiritual and the bodily,
believing that both needed attention and that both could take the other with
along with it. Today, she said, we have uplifted our souls and so our bodies.

We then suggested that we conclude our Bible study, as is our practice in
the ISB&WM, by being quite practical. Given that they had stated that their
experiences were not allowed any space in the church, what about them
writing their own versions of Job 3? We would then collate them and make
them available to churches, which would use them in their liturgies. They
like this idea and set to work. We concluded our time together with each
person reading or talking to their version of Job 3. Again, there was considerable diversity, and here is not the place to reproduce their contributions in
full. We need to return their 'laments' to them and make sure that they are
happy to have them made public. We are in the process of collating, typing
and translating them.

Their versions of Job 3 ranged from commitments to return to their
families, having fled their rejection but having found resources which now
enabled a return, to sustained interrogations of God, asking repeatedly
'Why?' to prayers asking for help to accept the virus, to requests for enough
life to support her sons, to probing questions about God's reputation as a
healer and as a God who intervenes.

Conclusion

We have promised to return to Job 3 when next we meet for Bible study,
which is every other time they meet. By the end of this Bible study we were
exhausted, and Bongi Zenele made us all take deep breaths. There was an
amazing sense of relief in the group to have spoken what had been spoken,
and yet it had also been traumatic to relive those first moments of being
informed that you are HIV-positive. Job chapter 3 had taken us back to this
moment, but also beyond it. This 'positive' reading of Job 3 now occupies

that vast space between diagnosis and death, providing resources to live 'positively'.

Notes

1. See, for example, Tinyiko S. Maluleke, 'The challenge of HIV/AIDS for theological education in Africa: towards an HIV/AIDS sensitive curriculum', *Missionalia* 29, 2001, pp. 125–43; Ronald Nicolson, '*God in AIDS?*, five years later', *Bulletin for Contextual Theology in Africa* 7.1, 2000, pp. 10–12.
2. Per Frostin, *Liberation theology in Tanzania and South Africa: a First World interpretation*, Lund 1988, p. 11.
3. Ibid., pp. 6–11.
4. Plumzile Zondi-Mabizela, 'Beating the odds to strut its stuff: the body of Christ sharpening its resources', paper read at the Church of Norway Kirkemotet, 17–22 November 2003, at Oslo, Norway; see also Gideon Byamugisha, Lucy Y. Steinitz, Glen Williams and Phumzile Zondi (eds), *Journeys of faith: church-based responses to HIV and AIDS in three southern African countries*, St Albans 2002.
5. The Institute of the Study of the Bible and Worker Ministry Project (ISB&WM) works with initiatives like the Treatment Action Campaign. Launched in 1998, the aims of the Treatment Action Campaign (TAC) include 'ensuring access to proper, affordable treatment for AIDS sufferers, preventing and eliminating new HIV infections and fostering HIV/AIDS treatment literacy', *Mail and Guardian*, 31 January to 6 February 2003, p. 8.
6. Gerald O. West, 'Reading the Bible in the light of HIV/AIDS in South Africa', *The Ecumenical Review* 55.4, 2003, pp. 335–44. In using the terms 'New Testament' and 'Old Testament' I am using the terms that are regularly used by the vast majority of Bible readers in South Africa. In using them I am not being insensitive to the concerns and baggage others have about these terms; rather, I am giving priority to my context and its (different) baggage.
7. Justin S. Ukpong, 'Popular readings of the Bible in Africa and implications for academic readings: report on the field research carried out on oral interpretations of the Bible in Port Harcourt Metropolis, Nigeria under the auspices of the Bible in Africa project, 1991–94', and Knut Holter, 'Old Testament scholarship in Sub-Saharan African north of the Limpopo river', both articles in G. O. West and M. W. Dube (eds), *The Bible in Africa: Transactions, Trajectories, and Trends*, Leiden 2000.
8. Justin S. Ukpong, 'Developments in biblical interpretation in Africa: historical and hermeneutical directions', in ibid.
9. This article is based on a paper I presented at a World Council of Churches Workshop on HIV/AIDS, Stigma and Discrimination, Kempton Park, South Africa, November 2003. I was asked to present a paper on a theology of compassion in the Old Testament.

10. Gunther H. Wittenberg, 'Job the farmer: the Judean *am-haretz* and the wisdom movement', *Old Testament Essays* 4, 1991, pp. 151–70. I place 'Israel' in inverted commas because I want to problematize this term, see Gerald O. West, 'Biblical scholars inventing Ancient Israel and "ordinary readers" of the Bible re-inventing Biblical Studies', *Old Testament Essays* 11, 1998, pp. 629–44.

11. Wittenberg, 'Job the farmer' (n.10).

12. Habakuki Y. Lwendo, *The significance of the doctrine of retribution in Old Testament Job for pastoral counselling in Aids*, Masters, School of Theology, University of Natal, Pietermaritzburg 2000.

13. Walter Brueggemann, 'Trajectories in Old Testament literature and the sociology of ancient Israel', in N. K. Gottwald and R. A. Horsley (eds),. *The Bible and Liberation: Political and Social Hermeneutics*, Maryknoll, NY 1993.

14. For some other attempts to read the book of Job in the context of HIV/AIDS see Johanna Stiebert, 'Does the Hebrew Bible have anything to tell us about HIV/AIDS?', *Missionalia* 29, 2001, pp. 174–85; Madipoane Masenya (ngwana' Mphahlele), 'Between unjust suffering and the "silent" God: Job and HIV/AIDS sufferers in South Africa', *Missionalia* 29, 2001, pp. 186–99.

15. For further discussion see David J. A. Clines, *Job 1–20*, Dallas 1989, 67–105 and Gustavo Gutiérrez, *On Job: God-talk and the Suffering of the Innocent*, Maryknoll, NY 1991, pp. 7–10.

16. The research of Quarraisha Abdool Karim shows that while infection rates (though still high) are stabilizing, mortality rates are rising rapidly. Death, therefore, is something the churches and society will have to deal with increasingly in the next decade (cited in Beverley G. Haddad, 'Synergies between bio-medical and social science research in the context of HIV/AIDS', *African Religious Health Assets Programme Report: Pietermaritzburg Colloquium 2003*, pp. 23–28). Pastoral care will have to adapt to this shift (see Stuart C. Bate [ed.], *Responsibility in a time of AIDS: a pastoral response by Catholic theologians and AIDS activists in Southern Africa*, Pietermaritzburg 2003; Kagiso B. Kgosikwena, 'Pastoral care and the dying process of people living with HIV/AIDS: speaking of God in a crisis', *Missionalia* 29,2001, 200–19; Edwina Ward, 'Enabling lay pastoral care and counselling of people living with AIDS: Clinical Pastoral Education as a training ground', *Bulletin for Contextual Theology in Africa* 7 [1], 2000, pp. 26–9), as will burial societies (see B. Ntombi Ngwenya, '"We are all believers": crisis in living conditions and the intervention of burial societies in Botswana', *Missionalia* 29, 2001, pp. 282–303).

17. Through the Siyaphila groups the ISB&WM has begun to rehabilitate the funerals of people who have died from AIDS-related illnesses. When one of their members dies, they approach the family and the church in order to plan an alternative type of funeral, a funeral in which the status of the deceased is recognized and honoured rather than hidden and shamed. During such a funeral, other members of the Solidarity Programme bear testimony to living

'positively', and so the funeral performs a partially educative function.

18. The group agreed that they would like to be acknowledged for their contributions, but decided that we should not identify who said what.

19. The discussion was facilitated by Bongi Zengele, given that the dominant language was isiZulu, but the formulations were often mine.

20. Elsa Tamez, 'A Letter to Job', in J. S. Pobee and B. von Wartenberg-Potter (eds), *New Eyes for Reading: Biblical and Theological Reflections by Women from the Third World*, Geneva 1986.

DOCUMENTATION

'Do not quench the Spirit' (I Thess.5.19): In memory of Karl Rahner (1904–1984)

HERMANN HÄRING

Last March Karl Rahner would have been 100 years old; he died 20 years ago. As one of the founders of *Concilium* he belonged to this journal from 1964 until his death, initially as director of the section on pastoral theology and then as an advisory member of the editorial committee. That is reason enough for commemorating him in *Concilium*. Certainly one can ask which theologians are important and which are not, but that is an unfair question. At least another theologian who meant a great deal for *Concilium* should be mentioned here: Yves Congar, who was also born in 1904 and without whom Catholic theology today is inconceivable.[1] But here we shall be remembering Karl Rahner.

I. Present all over the world

Karl Rahner is still present in the theology of the Roman Catholic church all over the world. He has continued to be remembered all over the world in recent months. The Pontifical Lateran University in Rome organized a congress, the University of Messina in Sicily an 'Academic Day'. The resepected Catholic journal *Avvenire* devoted a whole page to Rahner containing interviews with Ignazio Sanna (Rome), Rosino Gibellini (Brescia) and Silvano Zucal (Trent). The excellent study by I.Sanna[2] has had an important influence. Queriniana has also published an Italian translation of the well-known German introduction to Rahner's theology by Raffelt and Verweyen.[3] There has recently been a large international symposium on the role of theology in the twenty-first century at the Jesuit University of São Leopoldo in Brazil. The studies by Miranda (1975) and Oliviera (1984) continue to have a great influence.[4] The English Jesuit P.Endean has written a fine and very instructive article on the reception of Rahner in the English-language world for the German Jesuit journal *Stimmen der Zeit*.[5] He shows that dialogue with Rahner has been continuous over past decades and is still taking place. As in Germany, alongside the universal standard questions of theology,[6] two themes are central. These are methodological questions about 'transcendental theology',[7] which of course continue to have major consequences, and the question of the spirituality of the great theologian, which is markedly inspired by Ignatius of Loyola.[8]

In the theology of Spain the work and influence of Karl Rahner are presnt everywhere: the renewal before and after the Council is inconceivable without him. He is read, in books[9] and professional articles, even if in recent years there have been few monographs and detailed studies devoted to him.[10] Almost all his work has been translated. Jesús Aguerre deserves special thanks for translating the first seven volumes of *Schriften zur Theologie* with great sensitivity and competence.[11] In 1974 the Pontifical Comillas Univesity held a congress to mark Rahner's seventieth birthday, which was documented in a special volume.[12] To mark Rahner's centenary the well known and much read journal *Vida Nueva* has produced an interesting issue edited by J. R. García-Murga.

Some restraint can be detected in France. For next year the Institut catholique de Paris has planned a joint symposium on Rahner and Balthasar. Rahner is still read, but is noted only marginally. This is not least because with the exception of *Grundkurs des Glaubens* his texts are so difficult to get hold of. As a result a rather narrow and partial Rahner scholasticism has grown up which is largely limited to his transcendentalism and the question of the 'anonymous Christian'. Nevertheless some specialist dissertations have been produced in recent years.[13] Rahner's universalism and his approaches to a theology of the religions continue to exercise an influence, though this is not plainly visible.

Above all in Germany and Austria Rahner has been remembered over recent months in lectures and symposia, in seminaries, lectures and new books.[14] The Karl Rahner Academy in Cologne has issued invitations to demanding seminars, symposia and a variety of evening lectures.[15] All have been well attended.[16] The Jesuit journal *Stimmen der Zeit* has published a special issue on Rahner.[17] Other journals which attract a wide public that enjoys discussion have produced sometimes moving articles on Rahner's significance.[18] The big Rahner reader has been reissued, as have a well-known collection of prayers and those of his books which have found the largest readership. And there are the meditations on 'Prayer. A Need and a Blessing', given in Munich in the difficult year of 1946.[19] Of course this wave of interest meant a lot for the Karl Rahner Archive in Innsbruck,[20] which with great vigour devotes itself to historical research into and reconstruction of Rahner's theology, and which has already been able to present interesting results of its work.[21] Finally, of course, time and again intensive reference has been made to the editing of the Collected Works of Rahner: this is a mammoth project which is being advanced with high scholarly accuracy.[22]

II. A theology for today

It is amazing how intense interest continues to be in this theologian of the first hour. Not only are there debates on methodological questions and the limits and possibilities of his 'transcendental' theology. There are also discussions of Rahner's influence on the Second Vatican Council and on Catholic theology and on the form of the church today and – with growing intensity – there are discussions of the spiritual foundations of Rahner's thought. This is not a matter of chance, for no twentieth-century theologian has exercised such a lasting influence on German-language theology as Rahner. Nor has any theologian taken up such a wide range of theological questions and discussed them with unexpected openness.

Rahner's theological career began with questions about epistemology and the philosophy of religion. He became known at a very early stage for terms like 'supernatural existential' and 'hearers of the word'. But the systematic theologian who was intensively confronted with pastoral questions in Vienna during the Second World War (1939–1944) later showed a particular interest in pastoral theology. This pointed him in four directions.

1. First of all he grappled with the 'simple' questions of the faithful who wanted to understand the traditional structure of faith. So he did not hesitate to discuss at a high level questions of the sacraments, devotion to the Sacred Heart of Jesus, veneration of Mary and indulgences.

2. Then he thought it of prime importance that theology and the church should link up with a modern view of human beings: theology should learn to understand itself in terms of anthropology. Subject and autonomy, freedom and free self-surrender became key concepts of his thought.

3. Moreover, as a pupil of Heidegger (1934–36) and an expert on Kant,[23] as early as the 1940s he reacted very sensitively to the development of a secular society and a culture in which the question of God was gradually being forgotten. The church had to learn to look over the fences. The later controversial terms 'anonymous believer' and 'anonymous Christian' have their origin here.

4. Finally, for Rahner all questions and answers issued in a deep, unfathomable, almost passionate faith in the hidden God, which for him was a mystery that encounters and holds captive all men and women – expressly or unthematically. For him all ways led to this mystery. From his student

days Rahner must have been stamped with a very deep experience of God. His readers sensed this when they could no longer follow his often complicated reflections.

III. The breakthrough at the Council

Rahner's theological career, like those of many of his friends and opponents, took on a new quality from the moment that John XXIII convened the Second Vatican Council. For him too, 1962–1965 were years of a theological reorientation, an unprecedented international communication and quite unexpected possibilities of influencing the course and form of the church. It cannot be claimed that during these years Rahner reformulated his theology or fundamentally changed it; in any case, at the beginning of the Council he was already fifty-eight years old. But he was well prepared for the demands of the Council. Like so many others he engaged ceaselessly in endless conversations and speeches, in conferences, books and articles. At that time and in subsequent years he took the opportunity to reformulate many fundamental questions, work on which had been blocked for decades. Like Edward Schillebeeckx he allowed himself to be guided by what at first sight looked like an almost chaotic variety of individual theological questions. He wrote countless articles, often the fruit of lectures which – thank God – have all been collected in his *Theological Investigations* or other books.[24]

The central lines of Rahner's own fundamental thought crystallized for his readership only gradually. Strangely enough, the picture of the really serious theologian who is concentrating on the central themes grew only gradually. Here Rahner's complicated and for a long time also technical language worked like a filter which consistently sifted out many redundancies and also an excess of reminiscences of a scholastic theology that was passing away. The question which people put was always 'What does he really mean?' Neo-scholastic terminology, the jargon of Heidegger, the Kantian way of posing problems and an excessively complex sentence structure proved alienating. In addition – more as a result of circumstances than deliberately – Rahner engaged massively in theological politics. He conceived and edited the *Handbuch der Pastoraltheologie*,[25] the lexicon *Sacramentum Mundi*,[26] and above all the highly influential *Lexikon für Theologie und Kirche*,[27] the systematic theology of which bears the marks, almost exclusively, of Rahner's hand. From the beginning his fellow-Jesuits gave him great support. Soon, against his will, he founded a school, since he could not avoid polarizations around his person, nor did he.[28] Rome also took action against him, but this was stopped after the Council. Unfortunately it was later thought necessary to put Rahner's orthodoxy in doubt. Contemporaries like Hans Urs von Balthasar and Joseph Ratzinger could not stop launching massive attacks on this great thinker who was also a profound believer.[29]

IV. The hour for *Concilium*

For *Concilium* Karl Rahner was literally the man of the first hour. As early as 1958 the distinguished Dutch publisher Paul Brand had proposed to him that they should collaborate on a major international theological journal. At that time Paul Brand was looking (as he said later) for 'a powerful and open world theology, ready for renewal'. Rahner hesitated until Brand repeated his proposal on 21 November 1962 – Brand knows the precise date.[30] The Council had opened and the great opportunities and also the first confrontations were becoming evident. Rahner finally agreed to the plan, and he and Brand decided to involve Edward Schillebeeckx and Hans Küng in the work; soon they were also joined by Yves Congar. Rahner was a stroke of luck for *Concilium*. Together with Schillebeeckx he wrote the very first editorial with which *Concilium* introduced itself. From 1964 to 1969 he was director of the section on pastoral theology. From this time we are indebted to him for five issues which from the beginning had diverse and above all international content. They were on basic questions of pastoral theology (1965), mission (1966), unbelief (atheism) (1967), Christian proclamation (1968) and priesthood (1969). These themes are also reflected in his own articles. They discuss questions of the form of the church;[31] the proclamation and reformulation of the faith;[32] spirituality, unbelief and ideology;[33] and the new challenges of contemporary theology.[34]

Rahner made a last public appearance for *Concilium* in July 1970 at the international congress in Brussels. Those were memorable and turbulent days, in which for the first time liberation theology made public statements. Already by then he presented himself as the grand old man: no longer the man of these new movements but the one who in public could hold his protective hand over them. As at the Second Vatican Council, Rahner also did a great deal of work in the background for *Concilium*. He advised and inspired, adopted standpoints and mediated. In some respects he represented the 'old theology': to begin with he preferred to speak in Latin and was criticized for an incomprehensibly exotic language. But he also continually translated this language, its form and content, into the present. No speech left out the question how human freedom comes into play, and no plea for the problems of past theology forgot reference to a critical and self-critical translation into the present. Karl Rahner's thoughts were never 'finished'; he had come to realize how complex the problems were and to see ways in which a theology could abandon its Eurocentricity.

V. Reception and criticism

It is all the more regrettable that discussion of Karl Rahner in German has become a matter for insiders. Rahner's pupils (now grown older) and his defenders (who are refreshingly young) have lost sight of other continents and theological schools. It is understandable that Rahner's clash with Hans Küng is usually suppressed or kept quiet about, since it draws attention to a weak point in Rahner's theology which he never worked out. But it is less understandable that references to the *nouvelle théologie*, to Congar and Schillebeeckx, equally are made only rarely – as if Rahner had lived on an island and as if present-day theology was obligated to scholasticism for having saved its honour, as if grappling with the results of exegesis were not overdue. More thought is needed here. Rahner certainly attempted to build a bridge from classical metaphysics (and scholasticism) to a questioning approach which takes seriously human beings as they understand themselves today, as subject and freedom, autonomy and self-surrender at the same time. Despite all the attention to the 'historicity' of human beings, the concrete stories about Jesus, the church and theology in a variety of contexts never appear. There is a failure to see the degree to which a conservative policy in the church and theology appeals today to Rahner, the great guardian of metaphysical scholastic thought.

That makes it all the more salutary that *Stimmen der Zeit* published a refreshing article by the English Jesuit P. Endean which shows some signs of the open yet critical spirit of Anglo-Saxon discussion.[35] In it Rahner is not presented one-sidedly as the 'father of the faith', 'church teacher',[36] or 'the greatest witness to the faith in our time'. He is seen as a professional colleague, treated with fairness and the utmost respect, but at the same time drawn into open criticism. With the utmost brevity, Endean describes not only the reception of Karl Rahner in the English-speaking world but also the main lines of his criticism. He quotes the well-known American theologian Anne Carr, who presents Rahner as a 'bridge' between traditional theology and the new theology that is coming into being.[37] Obviously Rahner did not use his transcendental method and a historically responsible thought for mutual reconciliation.[38] His influence meant that the great attempts of the 1970s (reconciling narrative and belief in Christ, a historically responsible christology 'from below' and the great formulae of faith arising out of a culture dominated by metaphysics) were received only to a limited degree.

VI. 'In season and out of season'

In 1964, when *Concilium* was founded, Karl Rahner was already over sixty years of age. Because of his intellectual vitality that has often been overlooked. And it makes all the more amazing his constant openness to new approaches, even if he no longer played an active part in shaping them. Thus in the last decade of his life he became the wise old man who supported everyone. With his intellect, which was lively to the end, with good words and a number of interventions, to his utmost ability he helped all those whose youthful theological concerns showed him some liveliness of spirit. In a last greeting, a few months before his death, now looking back on '190 issues of *Concilium*', he made some remarks which are still highly topical today: ' I believe that the age of the church as the church of the whole world, of all the cultures and of world civilization, has begun to exist. It has begun despite all the reactionary tendencies of today and despite all the dangers everywhere inherent in a world dominated by technological rationality. If the church must nevertheless be the one church of God's most radical self-offering in Jesus Christ, there must be theological journals in this one world church which strive to reflect and articulate this new situation of the church, its faith and its theology.' So for Rahner, 'it is obvious that the pluralism in the theology of the world church, which today is inevitable and should be accepted as a strength, needs an international journal to be a meeting place in which theologians from all over the world can collaborate. If in practice such an international theological journal exists only in *Concilium*, even someone who would like to see other journals of this sort, and regards them as necessary, would want to wish *Concilium* continued existence and successful development, even though no journal of this sort has the promise of immortality.'[39] This description of the situation in the church and of the task of *Concilium* has not changed.

That particularly in his latter years Rahner sometimes aroused the anger of a stagnating and authoritarian church leadership is insufficiently unknown and arouses our sympathy. But an Ignatian spirituality and thus trust in the power of the spirit were far more important, and these continued to shape his theology to the end.[40] He helped the church to go forward in all its crises. He did not need cautions from the church authorities or endless admonitions of the kind that have been repeated time and again since the 1980s and are of no use to a church in need of and ready for reform. Rahner described his way of thinking as 'transcendental theology': whether we are secular or religious, believers or atheists, with every act of knowledge we are with God, for our spirit is always open to the infinite.[41] Even those who do not believe that they can perceive anything hear God's words simply if they listen seriously to themselves, to their fellow human beings and to reality.[42] Furthermore they always perceive Christ himself here. We need only listen to reality. With this approach Karl Rahner built a bridge from classical metaphysics (and scholasticism) to a questioning which takes human beings (subject and freedom, autonomy and self surrender) seriously.

'Do not quench the spirit' (I Thess 5.19): this favourite saying of Karl Rahner's is the most important call that *Concilium* has learned from him. Hopefully it will not forget it in the future.

Translated by John Bowden

Notes

1. A memorial to Yves Congar (1904–1995) is planned at the Dominican cultural centre in Pistoia, Tuscany.
2. I. Sanna, *Teologia come esperienza di Dio. La prospettiva cristologica di Karl Rahner*, Brescia 1997.
3. Albert Raffelt and Hansjürgen Verweyen, *Leggere Karl Rahner*, Brescia 2004.
4. Mário de França Miranda, *O mistério de Deus em nossa vida: A doutrina trinitária de Karl Rahner*, São Paulo 1975; Manfredo Araújo de Oliveira, *Filosofia transcendental e religião: Ensaio sobre a filosofia da religião em Karl Rahner*, São Paulo 1984.
5. P. Endean, 'Karl Rahner im englischsprachigen Raum', in *Stimmen der Zeit* (ed.), *Karl Rahner – 100 Jahre, Spezial 1*, with contributions by M. Maier, etc., Freiburg 2004, pp. 57–74.
6. A general introduction by G. Vass, *Understanding Karl Rahner* (5 vols), London 1985. For his christology and doctrine of grace see L. J. O'Donovan (ed.), *A World of Grace. An Introduction to the Theme and Foundations of Karl Rahner's Theology*, New York 1987; J. H. P. Wong, *Logos-Symbol in the Christology of Karl Rahner*, Rome 1984.
7. There is an important study by A. E. Carr, *The Theological Method of Karl Rahner*, Missoula 1977.
8. At an early stage see H. D. Egan, *The Spiritual Exercises and the Ignatian Mystical Horizon*, St Louis 1976; later the more specialist study by C. A. Callahan, *Karl Rahner's Spirituality of the Pierced Heart. A Reinterpretation of the Devotion to the Sacred Heart*, Lanham 1985; finally D. Marmion, *A Spirituality of Everyday Faith. A Theological Investigation of the Notion of Spirituality in Karl Rahner*, Louvain 1998; P. Endean, *Karl Rahner and Ignatian Spirituality*, Oxford 2001.

9. Jésus Avelino González García (Jesús A. de la Pienda), *Antropología trascendental de Karl Rahner*, Oviedo 1982; Secretariado Trinitario, *Teología trinitaria de K. Rahner*, Salamanca 1987; Jose Luis Rodríguez Molinero, *La Antropología filosófica de Karl Rahner*, Salamanca 1979; J. R. García-Murga, *Intimidad con Dios y servicio al prójimo. A la luz de la teología de Rahner*, Madrid 1968; there are also numerous doctoral studies which were supervised by Kart Rahner.

10. Avelino de Luis Ferreras, *La incomprensibilidad de Dios en Karl Rahner*, Salamanca 1995; Gonzalo J. Zarazaga, *Trinidad y comunión: la teología trinitaria de Karl Rahner y la pregunta por sus rasgos hegelianos*, Bilbao 1999; A. Cordovilla Pérez, *Gramática de la Encarnación. La creación en Cristo en la teología de K. Rahner y H. Urs von Balthasar*, Madrid 2004.

11. They are being reissued by Editiones Cristiandad; however, no note is being taken of the German critical edition.

12. *Teología y mundo contemporáneo. Homenaje a Karl Rahner en su 70 cumpleaños*, Madrid 1975: the appreciation of Rahner by A. Álvarez Bolado (pp. 27–34) is important.

13. Evelyne Maurice, *La christologie de Karl Rahner*, Paris 1995; Yves Tourenne, *La théologie du dernier Rahner, 'Aborder au sans-rivage'*, Cogitatio fidei 187, Paris 1995; Vincent Holzer, *Le Dieu Trinité dans l'histoire. Le différend théologique Balthasar – Rahner*, Cogitatio fidei 187, Paris 1995.

14. The best and most up to date introduction is H. Vorgrimler, *Karl Rahner. Gotteserfahrung in Leben und Denken*, Darmstadt 2004. Other important introductory literature includes: B. J. Hilberath, *Karl Rahner. Gottgeheimnis Mensch*, Mainz 1995; E. Klinger, *Das absolute Geheimnis im Alltag entdecken. Zur spirituellen Theologie Karl Rahners*, Würzburg 1994; K.H. Neufeld, *Die Brüder Rahner. Eine Biographie*, Freiburg 1994; A. Raffelt – H. Verweyen, *Karl Rahner*, Munich 1997; K. H. Weger, *Karl Rahner. Eine Einführung in sein theologisches Denken*, Freiburg 1986.

15. http://www.kath.de/akademie/rahner/

16. A comprehensive bibliography has just appeared, but unfortunately limited to the German language area: H. Vorgrimler, 'Zur bleibenden Aktualität Karl Rahners', *Theologische Revue* 2004.2, pp. 91–100.

17. *Stimmen der Zeit* (n.5).

18. G. Pöhlmann, 'Namenloses Geheimnis. Das ganze Glück, der ganze Friede, die ganze Freiheit: Karl Rahner in memoriam', *zeitzeichen* 3/2004, pp. 52–4; *Orientierung, Herder-Korrespondenz* etc. See also P. Endean, 'A Message yet to be Heard', *The Tablet*, 6 March 2004, p. 15; R. Siebenrock, 'Von der Mitte in die Weite. Karl Rahner aus der Sicht der "Generation danach"', *Christ in der Gegenwart 56* (9 May 2004).

19. K. Lehmann and A. Raffelt (eds), *Karl Rahner, Lesebuch*, Freiburg 2004; K. Rahner, *Gebete des Lebens* (ed. A. Raffelt, with an introduction by K. Lehmann), Freiburg 2004; K. Rahner, *Von der Not und dem Segen des Gebetes* (with an introduction by R. Hubert und R. A. Siebenrock), Freiburg 2004.

20. The archive was founded in 1985. It collects and systematically archives the literary legacy of Karl Rahner (texts, letters, biographical documents), *Dokumente zum 2. Vatikanischen Konzil.* The documents of his brother Hugo Rahner have a special place, as do those of J. A. Jungmann with whom Karl Rahner had a close relationship (cf. www/ theol.uibk.ac.at/forsch/rahnerarchiv-1.html). Publications which are largely in debt to the archive include: A. R. Batlogg et al., *Der Denkweg Karl Rahners. Quellen – Erinnerungen – Perspektiven*, Mainz 2003; R. Siebenrock (ed.), *Karl Rahner in der Diskussion. Erstes und zweites Innsbrucker Karl-Rahner-Symposion: Themen – Referate – Ergebnisse*, Innsbruck and Vienna 2001.

21. Batlogg et al., *Denkweg* (n.20).

22. Karl Rahner, *Sämtliche Werke*, ed. Karl-Rahner-Stiftung, under the direction of K. Lehmann, J.B. Metz, K.-H. Neufeld, A. Raffelt und H. Vorgrimler, Freiburg, Solothurn and Düsseldorf 1995ff. The work is planned to comprise 32 volumes.

23. Rahner's epistemological study *Geist in Welt. Zur Metaphysik der endlichen Erkenntnis bei Thomas von Aquin*, Innsbruck 1939, is fundamental. The second edition revised by J. B. Metz (Munich 1957) is widely circulated.

24. The series *Schriften zur Theologie*, Einsiedeln, Zurich and Cologne, comprises 16 volumes (1954–1984). The later compact systematic work *Grundkurs des Glaubens, Einführung in den Begriff des Christentums*, Freiburg 1976, the language and content of which are very dense, later became important. A special edition, the eighth, appeared in 1997; it is now published as Vol.26 of the Sämtlichen Werke.

25. 5 vols, Freiburg 1970–1972.

26. 4 vols, Freiburg 1967–1969.

27. Second edition, 10 volumes, 3 volumes with Council documents, 1 Index volume, Freiburg 1957–1967.

28. K. Rahner (ed.), *Zum Problem der Unfehlbarkeit. Antworten auf die Anfrage von Hans Küng*, Freiburg 1971; this includes an article by Rahner, 'Kritik an Hans Küng. Zur Frage der Unfehlbarkeit theologischer Sätze', pp. 27–48. Cf. also the tendency to exclude the problem of demythologizing in 'Heilsauftrag der Kirche und Humanisierung der Welt', in *Schriften zur Theologie* X, Einsiedeln 1972, pp. 547–67. For Rahner's ambivalence to the claim of exegetes to present a historically responsible christology see 'Bemerkungen zur Bedeutung der Geschichte Jesu für die katholische Dogmatik', ibid., pp. 215–26. This could also be demonstrated with ecclesiology: K. Rahner, 'Zur Ekklesiologie', in H. U. von Balthasar et al., *Diskussion über Hans Küngs 'Christ sein'*, Mainz 1976, pp. 105–11. His whole indecision over a new approach becomes clear in his request to readers to read Küng carefully and (above all) critically. In short, we still need an account of Rahner's perplexity over theological problems which reached Catholic theology only after the 1970s; it would not damage Rahner's reputation but rather enhance it.

29. The criticism is already evident in H. U. von Balthasar, *Cordula oder der Ernstfall*, Einsiedeln 1966.

30. P. Brand and H. Häring, 'Aggiornamento als wissenschaftliches Projekt. Über Aufträge und Programmatik der Internationalen Zeitschrift für Theologie "CONCILIUM"', in H. Häring and K.-J. Kuschel (eds), *Hans Küng. Neue Horizonte des Glaubens und Denkens. Ein Arbeitsbuch*, Munich 1993, pp. 779–94.

31. 'Observations on Episcopacy in the Light of Vatican II' (1965/3, pp. 10–14); 'What Is the Theological Starting Point for a Definition of the Priestly Ministry?' (1969/3, pp. 43–6); 'Some Observations on the Article by Hans Heimerl' (1966/3, p. 73).

32. 'Demythologization and the Sermon', 1968/3, pp. 12–20; 'Preaching and Preaching Aids: Introductory Remarks', 1968/3, p. 57; 'In Search of a Short Formula of the Christian Faith', 1967/3, pp. 36–42; 'Christology Today, Instead of a Conclusion', 1982/3, pp. 73–7.

33. 'Christianity and Ideology', 1965/6, pp. 23–32; 'The Teaching of the Second Vatican Council on Atheism?', 1967/3, p. 7–24 ; 'Ervaring van de Geest en existentiële beslissing', in *Leven uit de geest. Theologische peilingen aangeboden aan Edward Schillebeeckx*, Hilversum 1974, pp. 150–61; 'Dimensions of Martyrdom: A Plea for the Broadening of a Classical Concept', 1983/3, pp. 9–11.

34. 'Evolution and Original Sin', 1967/6, pp. 30–5; 'Pluralism in Theology and the Oneness of the Church's Profession of Faith', 1969/6, pp. 49–58; 'Was ist die christliche Botschaft?', in *Berichtband zum Kongress von CONCILIUM "Die Zukunft der Kirche"*, Zürich and Mainz 1970, pp. 74–7; 'Orthodoxy and Freedom in Theology', 1971/6, pp. 90–104.

35. Endean, 'Karl Rahner im englischsprachigen Raum' (n.5); his *Karl Rahner and Ignatian Spirituality* (n.8) is also important.

36. It should also be mentioned that Rahner has been immortalized as a 'teacher of the church' in a window in Grace Cathedral, San Francisco (1967) alongside Karl Barth und Paul Tillich. Cf. www.gracecathedral.org.

37. 'In the dialectic between past and present experience Rahner seeks to maintain the continuity which for him is Roman Catholic tradition. He is recognized as the bridge or transitional figure between the old in the Catholic tradition and the new which has not yet taken shape.' See 'Theology and experience in the thought of Karl Rahner', *Journal of Religion* 53, 1973, 359–76: 376.

38. N. Knoepffler, *Der Begriff 'transzendental' bei Karl Rahner. Zur Frage seiner Kantischen Herkunft*, Innsbruck and Vienna 1993.

39. '"In Season and Out of Season"', 1983/10, pp. 88–9.

40. K. P. Fischer, *Der Mensch als Geheimnis. Die Anthropologie Karl Rahners*, Freiburg 1974; vgl. Endean, 'Karl Rahner im englischsprachigen Raum' (n.5).

41. J. Herzgsell, *Dynamik des Geistes. Ein Beitrag zum anthropologischen Transzendenzbegriff von Karl Rahner*, Innsbruck and Vienna 2000.

42. Karl Rahner, *Hearers of the Word*, New York 1969.

Articles in Concilium in English by Karl Rahner

1965/1: 'General Introduction' (with E. Schillebeeckx, pp. 3–4)

1965/3: 'Observations on Episcopacy in the Light of Vatican II' (pp. 10–14)

1965/6: 'Christianity and Ideology' (pp. 23–32)

1966/3: 'Some Observations on the Article by Hans Heimerl' (p. 73)

1967/3: 'The Teaching of the Second Vatican Council on Atheism?' (pp. 5–13)

'In Search of a Short Formula of the Christian Faith' (pp. 36–42)

1967/6: 'Evolution and Original Sin' (pp. 30–5)

1968/3: 'Demythologization and the Sermon' (pp. 12–20)

'Preaching and Preaching Aids: Introductory Remarks' (with Karl Lehmann, p. 57)

1969/3: 'What Is the Theological Starting Point for a Definition of the Priestly Ministry?' (pp. 43–6)

1969/6: 'Pluralism in Theology and the Oneness of the Church's Profession of Faith' (pp. 49–58)

1971/6: 'Orthodoxy and Freedom in Theology' (pp. 90–104)

153 (1982/3): 'Christology Today (Instead of a Conclusion)' (pp. 73–7)

163 (1983/3): 'Dimensions of Martyrdom: A Plea for the Broadening of a Classical Concept' (pp. 9–11)

170 (1983/10): '"In Season and Out of Season"' (pp. 88–9)

Contributors

ELLEN VAN WOLDE was born in The Netherlands in 1954 and educated at Nijmegen University (PhD 1989), the Pontifical Biblical Institute in Rome, and the University of Bologna. Since 1992 she has been Professor of the Exegesis of the Old Testament and Hebrew at the Theological Faculty of the University of Tilburg. She is programme leader of the international research project *Knowing and Experiencing Job* at the University of Tilburg. She has contributed several articles to journals and books on Genesis, Samuel, Ruth, Job, and monotheism, as well as on methodology (linguistics, semiotics, literary criticism and cognitive studies). Among her books are: *Words become Worlds. Semantic Studies of Genesis 1–11*, Leiden and Boston: E. J. Brill 1993; *Stories of the Beginning*, London: SCM Press 1996; *Mr and Mrs Job*, London: SCM Press 1997; *Ruth and Naomi*, London: SCM Press 1997; she has also edited *Narrative Syntax and the Hebrew Bible*, Leiden and Boston: E. J. Brill, 1997, 2002 and *Job 28. Cognition in Context*, Leiden: E. J. Brill, 2003.

Address: Tilburg Faculty of Theology, POBox 9130, NL-5000 HC Tilburg, The Netherlands
E-mail: E.J.vWolde@uvt.nl

ALBERT KAMP was born in the Netherlands in 1968 and educated in biblical studies at Nijmegen University and Tilburg University (PhD 2002). He is at present a researcher at the Theological Faculty of the University of Tilburg and teacher of biblical studies at the Fontys Hogeschool Hengelo. His current research is embedded in the international programme *Knowing and Experiencing Job* of the Tilburg Faculty of Theology and focuses on the application of cognitive linguistics in the field of biblical studies. He has published on Jonah and Job, including *Inner Worlds. A Cognitive Linguistic Approach of the Book of Jonah*, Leiden and Boston: E. J. Brill 2004, and 'World Building in Job 28: A Case of Conceptual Logic', in E. J.van Wolde (ed.), *Job 28. Cognition in Context*, Leiden and Boston: E. J. Brill 2003.

Address: Stockholmstraat 121, 7559 JS Hengelo, The Netherlands
E-mail: A.H.Kamp@uvt.nl

PIERRE VAN HECKE was born in Belgium in 1970. He studied at the Catholic University of Louvain and the Hebrew University of Jerusalem. In 2000 he gained his doctoral degree in biblical sciences at the Louvain Faculty of Arts. Since then, he has been lecturer of Hebrew at the Tilburg Faculty of Theology, where he is also working for a doctorate in theology. He contributed to the new interconfessional Dutch Bible translation (NBV) and has published several articles on biblical metaphor and on the book of Job in different international journals and books, including 'Searching for and exploring wisdom. A cognitive-semantic approach to the Hebrew verb *'haqar'* in Job 28', in E. J.van Wolde (ed.), *Job 28. Cognition in Context*, Leiden and Boston: E. J. Brill 2003, pp. 139–62; 'Job xii:18. Text and Interpretation', *Vetus Testamentum*, 54 (2004). A book edited by him, *Metaphors in the Hebrew Bible*, BETL, Leuven: University Press – Peeters will appear during 2004.

Address: Tilburg Faculty of Theology, P.O. Box 9130, NL-5000 HC Tilburg, The Netherlands
E-mail: P.J.P.vanHecke@uvt.nl

NORMAN C. HABEL was born in Australia and is currently Professorial Fellow at Flinders University, Melbourne. He has long been involved in issues of biblical interpretation and social justice. Among his writings is a major commentary on the biblical book of Job (*The Book of Job: A Commentary*, London: SCM Press and Philadelphia: Westminster Press 1985). He has also published *Reconciliation: Searching for Australia's Soul*, a work that traces our journey from being racists to advocates of reconciliation. His recent research includes *The Earth Bible* (Sheffield University Press/Continuum), a five-volume international project reading the Bible from the perspective of justice for Earth. He is concerned that we, as human beings, re-connect with Earth as a sanctuary, a living planet and an expression of God's presence. Currently he is exploring ways in which the church in Australia can introduce a four-week season of creation into the church year. On the Queen's Birthday, 2003, he was made a Member of the Order of Australia (AM) for 'services to education and the development of courses in religious studies in tertiary institutions in Australia, to reconciliation and social justice, and to the environment'.

E-mail: Nhabel@senet.com.au

DAVID J.A. CLINES was born in Australia and is Research Professor in the Department of Biblical Studies in the University of Sheffield, where he has taught since 1964. He holds the degrees of BA (in Classical Languages) from the University of Sydney, MA (in Semitic Languages) from the University of Cambridge, and PhD (honoris causa) from the University of Amsterdam. His books include *The Theme of the Pentateuch* (1978), *Ezra, Nehemiah, Esther* (1984), *The Esther Scroll* (1984), *What does Eve Do To Help?* (1990) and *Interested Parties: The Ideology of Writers and Readers of the Hebrew Bible* (1995); many of his articles are collected in two volumes, *On the Way to the Postmodern: Old Testament Essays, 1967–1998* (1998) (all published by Sheffield Academic Press). He published the first volume of his commentary on Job (*Job 1–20*) in the Word Biblical Commentary series in 1989, and the second and third volumes are expected this year from Thomas Nelson, Nashville. He is editor of the eight-volume *Dictionary of Classical Hebrew* (Sheffield: Sheffield Academic Press 1993–) of which the sixth volume will be published this year.

Address: Dept of Biblical Studies, University of Sheffield, Sheffield S10 2TN, UK
E-mail: d.clines@sheffield.ac.uk

SASKIA WENDEL was born in Germany in 1964 and gained her doctorate and habilitation at the Theological Faculty of the University of Tilburg, The Netherlands, where she is Professor of Systematic Theology with a focus on metaphysics and the philosophy of religion. Important publications include: *Jean-Francois Lyotard. Aisthetisches Ethos*, Munich 1997; *Affektiv und inkarniert. Ansätze Deutscher Mystik als subjekttheoretische Herausforderung*, Regensburg 2002; *Feministische Ethik zur Einführung*, Hamburg 2003; *Christliche Mystik. Eine Einführung*, Regensburg 2004; *Jüdische Traditionen in der Philosophie des 20. Jahrhunderts* (edited with J. Valentin), Darmstadt 2000; *Unbedingtes Verstehen? Fundamentaltheologie zwischen Erstphilosophie und Hermeneutik* (edited with J. Valentin), Regensburg 2001.

Address: Tilburg Faculty of Theology, P.O. Box 9130, NL-5000 HC Tilburg, The Netherlands
E-mail: S.K.A.Wendel@uvt.nl

HERMANN HÄRING was born in 1937 and studied theology in Münich and Tübingen; between 1969 and 1980 he worked at the Institute of Ecumenical Research in Tübingen; since 1980 he has been Professor of Dogmatic Theology at the Catholic University of Nijmegen. His books include *Kirche und Kerygma. Das Kirchenbild in der Bultmannschule*, 1972; *Die Macht des Bösen. Das Erbe Augustins*, 1979; *Zum Problem des Bösen in der Theologie*,

1985; *Hans Küng. Breaking Through*, London 1998; *Das Böse in der Welt*, 1999. He was co-editor of the *Wörterbuch des Christentums*, 1988, and has written articles on ecclesiology and christology, notably for *Tijdschrift voor Theologie*.

Address: Katholieke Universiteit, Faculteit des Godgeleerdheit, Erasmusgebouw, Erasmusplein 1, 6525 HT Nijmegen, The Netherlands

JAN JANS was born in Belgium in 1954 and studied theology at the Katholieke Universiteit Leuven. He gained his doctorate in moral theology in 1990. Since 1991 he has been lecturer in moral theology at Tilburg Faculty of Theology, and since 2001/2002 visiting professor at St Augustine College of South Africa. His field of research includes questions of fundamental moral theology as well as medical ethics and media ethics. Some recent publications are: *La régulation des naissances à Vatican II : une semaine de crise*. Un dossier en 40 documents constitué, introduit et commenté par Jan Grootaers and Jan Jans, Annua Nuntia Lovaniensia XLIII, Leuven 2002; '"Sterbehilfe" in den Niederlanden und Belgien. Rechtslage, Kirchen und ethische Diskussion'. *Zeitschrift für evangelische Ethik* 46, 2002, pp. 283–300; 'Christian Ethics: On the Difficult Dialectics between Faith and Ethics', *Australian Journal of Theology*, February 2004/2. [http://dlibrary.acu.edu.au/research/theology/ejournal/aejt_2/Jan_Jans.htm].

Address: Tilburg Faculty of Theology, P.O. Box 9130, NL-5000 HC Tilburg, The Netherlands
E-mail: Jan.Jans@uvt.nl

RON PIRSON was born in the Netherlands and educated at the Theological Faculty of the University of Tilburg (PhD 2000). He is currently lecturer in Old Testament at the Theological Faculty of the University of Tilburg. His English publications are on the story of Joseph and his brothers – his most recent being *The Lord of the Dreams. A Semantic and Literary Analysis of Genesis 37–50*, JSOTS 355, Sheffield: Sheffield Academic Press 2002 – and the writings of J.R.R. Tolkien. At present he is writing a Dutch commentary on the book of Genesis.

Address: Tilburg Faculty of Theology, P.O. Box 9130, NL-5000 HC Tilburg, The Netherlands
E-mail: R.W.J.Pirson@uvt.nl

ELSA TAMEZ was born in Mexico in 1950 and received her Doctor's Degree in Theology from the University of Lausanne, Switzerland. She received her Licenciate in Theology in 1979 from the Latin American Biblical Seminary, and a Licenciate in Literature and Linguistics at the National University of Costa Rica in1986. She is a faculty member of the Latin American Biblical University in Costa Rica and a member of the team of researchers of the Ecumenical Department of Investigation (DEI) in Costa Rica. Among her publications are: *Diccionario conciso Griego-Español* (1978); *Bible of the Oppressed* (1982); *The Scandalous Message of James* (1989); *Amnesty of Grace* (1993); and *When the Horizons Close: Rereading Ecclesiastes* (2000). She has also edited: *Against Machismo* (1987); *Women's Rereading of the Bible* (1988); and *Through Her Eyes; Women Theologians from Latin America* (1989).

Address: Universidad Bíblica Latinoamericana, Apartado 901–1000, San José, Costa Rica
E-mail: Eltamez@amnet.co.cr

GERALD WEST was born in South Africa and teaches Old Testament/ Hebrew Bible and African Biblical Hermeneutics in the School of Theology and Religion, University of KwaZulu-Natal. He is also Director of the Institute for the Study of the Bible and Worker Ministry Project, a project in which socially engaged biblical scholars and ordinary African readers of the Bible from poor, working-class and marginalized communities collaborate for social transformation. Among his West recent publications are *The Academy of the Poor: Towards a Dialogical Reading of the Bible*, Sheffield: Sheffield Academic Press 1999, reprinted Pietermaritzburg: Cluster Publications 2003, and a volume edited with Musa Dube, *The Bible in Africa: Transactions, Trajectories and Trends*, Leiden/Boston: E. J. Brill 2000.

E-mail: West@nu.ac.za

BONGI ZENGELE was born in South Africa and is the co-ordinator of the Solidarity Programme for People Living with HIV/AIDS within the Institute for the Study of the Bible and Worker Ministry Project. She is one of the founders of the Siyaphila support groups for people living with HIV and AIDS, who meet regularly to do contextual Bible study together and to share other resources. She is currently completing her Masters degree.

Concilium Subscription Information

February   2004/1: *Original Sin*

April   2004/2: *Rethinking Europe*

June   2004/3: *The Structural Betrayal of Trust*

October   2004/4: *Job's God*

December   2004/5: *A Different World is Possible*

New subscribers: to receive *Concilium 2004* (five issues) anywhere in the world, please copy this form, complete it in block capitals and send it with your payment to the address below.

Please enter my subscription for *Concilium 2004*

Individuals	Institutions
____ £32.50 UK/Rest of World	____ £48.50 UK/Rest of World
____ $63.00 North America	____ $93.50 North America

Please add £17.50/$33.50 for airmail delivery

Payment Details:

Payment must accompany all orders and can be made by cheque or credit card

I enclose a cheque for £/$ _____ Payable to SCM-Canterbury Press Ltd

Please charge my Visa/MasterCard (Delete as appropriate) for £/$ _____

Credit card number ....

Expiry date ....

Signature of cardholder ....

Name on card ....

Telephone .... E-mail ....

Send your order to *Concilium*, SCM-Canterbury Press Ltd
9–17 St Albans Place, London N1 ONX, UK
Tel +44 (0)20 7359 8033 Fax +44 (0)20 7359 0049
E-Mail: office@scm-canterburypress.co.uk

Customer service information:
All orders must be prepaid. Subscriptions are entered on an annual basis (i.e. January to December) No refunds on subscriptions will be made after the first issue of the Journal has been despatched. If you have any queries or require information about other payment methods, please contact our Customer services department.